INTRODUCTION TO ENGLISH LANGUAGE

Related titles from Macmillan

Introduction to English Language

N. F. Blake and Jean Moorhead

MACMILLAN

First published 1993 by
MACMILLAN PRESS LTD
Houndmills, Basingstoke, Hampshire RG21 2XS
and London
Companies and representatives
throughout the world

ISBN 0–333–57302–1 hardcover
ISBN 0–333–57303–X paperback

A catalogue record for this book is available
from the British Library.

10   9   8   7   6   5
02   01   00   99   98   97

Printed in Hong Kong

Contents

Acknowledgements

The authors and publishers gratefully acknowledge permission to reproduce material from the following works:

BBC Enterprises Ltd for a recipe from *Delia Smith's Complete Cookery Course*, BBC Books.

British Broadcasting Corporation, The Mental Health Foundation and Anthony Clare for his appeal on behalf of The Mental Health Foundation on Radio 4, 3 February 1991.

Carnell Ltd for 'How to talk to your cat' advertisement.

Casio Electronics Co. Ltd for 'Rap-1' advertisement.

Rosica Colin Ltd on behalf of the author for an extract from *The Loneliness of the Long Distance Runner* by Alan Sillitoe, copyright © Alan Sillitoe 1959, 1987.

Faber & Faber Ltd and Harcourt Brace & Company for an excerpt from *The Spire* by William Golding. Copyright © 1964, renewed 1992, by William Golding.

Little, Brown & Company (UK) Ltd for extracts from *Cooking for Special Occasions*, by Mrs Cozens.

Newspaper Publishing plc for material from *The Independent*, October 1991; 'Sacked preacher to reclaim citadel of the Lord' by David Nicholson-Lord, *The Independent*, February 1992; and '"Kidneys for sale" business may open', *The Independent*, 30 January 1989.

Peugeot Talbot for 'The perfect car for anyone between 50 and 70' advertisement.

Syndication International Ltd for 'Kidney dealer rumpus', *Daily Mirror*, 30 January 1989.

Every effort has been made to trace all the copyright-holders, but if any have been inadvertently overlooked the publishers will be pleased to make the necessary arrangement at the first opportunity.

Introduction

Imagine the two sentences '*E were right gormless* and *He was absolutely stupid*. What would you say about them? You might say that both of them are English and both mean more or less the same thing. You might also say that people react to these sentences in different ways. The second represents 'Standard English',* that variety of English used in writing and by educated people, whereas the first occurs only in the speech of some people and would be considered by many as 'non-standard'. As speakers of the language we recognise that there are differences in these two sentences and we make assumptions about speakers according to the way they speak, just as we make certain assumptions about people from the way they dress. But what are these differences and how can they be described? To start with, we can see that '*E* in the first sentence corresponds to *He* in the second; this is a difference in spelling which represents a difference in pronunciation because *h* may be dropped at the beginning of a word. There is a difference in the second word between *were* and *was* even though both have the same person *(H)e* who is being discussed. This could be said to be a difference in grammar, for some speakers of English would use *were* only after a word like *They*, meaning 'more than one'. Finally, the expression *right gormless* could be said to mean the same as *absolutely stupid*, though the words are different so that here we are dealing with a difference in vocabulary.

These two sentences differ in pronunciation (sounds, which in writing have to be represented by the spellings), grammar (the relationship between words) and vocabulary (the choice of words). All these features are present in any sentence in English. But if we want to describe these features in any detail and compare them with those in other sentences, we need to refer to the various categories and elements that go to make up pronunciation/writing, grammar, and vocabulary. This is what we do in Chapter 1,

---

*Remember to consult the Glossary of Linguistic Terms (p. 159) for terms you are not familiar with.

Describing the Structure and Sounds of English. There we outline
the make-up of an English sentence, what elements occur in it and in
what orders we expect to find them, as well as the various sounds
used in English. Before we can describe how English is used or
acquired, we need to have some means of talking about these
elements, which means learning some of the technical words to
describe the grammar and the sounds of language. *Grammar* is a
word that tends to frighten some people, but that is partly because it
is often connected with good grammar and speaking properly. From
the two sentences quoted in the last paragraph, you will have seen
that every sentence in English has grammar no matter whether it is
called 'standard' or 'non-standard'. For us grammar is simply the
means of describing how a language works and the terms that are
necessary to undertake a description of any variety of language. You
could not talk about clothes unless you know what is meant by *shirt*,
skirt, *blouse* and *trousers*, but to know the meaning of these words
does not imply you think a blouse is better than a shirt; these words
simply provide you with the means of talking about different forms
of clothing. The same applies to the words which are used to talk
about grammar: they enable you to talk about different varieties of
language in a sensible and an intelligible way.

Just as there are different ways of talking and writing about
clothes and fashion, so there are different ways of approaching
the grammar of language. Grammar has been a subject of debate
and investigation from the time of the Greeks in the sixth century
BC. The terminology which they and after them the Romans
developed remained the principal way of discussing the grammar
of English till the twentieth century and is sometimes referred to as
'traditional grammar'. Any grammatical terminology you learn
before you are sixteen will almost certainly be a form of traditional
grammar. In the twentieth century different types of grammar and
associated terminologies have been put forward by linguistic
researchers, but these have not been very helpful in dealing with
language in use. It is not our intention to teach you different
grammatical terminologies; we want you to learn the terminology
of one grammar to enable you to discuss such topics as language
acquisition and historical change in English. As the only terminology you are likely to be familiar with, if you know any at all, is that
of traditional grammar, we have decided in Chapter 1 to present a
terminology which is a modified and up-dated form of traditional
grammar. If you want a more advanced grammar and terminology,

you will find references to books you could use in the Suggestions for Further Reading on p. 170. But the terminology we put forward in Chapter 1 is concerned solely with the constituent parts of a sentence and the sounds of English.

When you have a grasp of the make-up of an English sentence and the sounds of English it is possible to approach Chapters 2–4 in a more informed way. These deal with Language Acquisition, Language Change, and Language Variety and the Social Context. Chapter 4 is slightly different from Chapters 2 and 3, which is why it comes at the end. Earlier we referred to standard and non-standard English, and many people regard Standard English as correct English. It is certainly the variety which is taught to foreign learners of English and, in its written form, it represents the form which is found in most types of writing – school text-books, government documents, newspapers and literature. But Standard English is only one variety among the many varieties of English, though it has acquired a special position among these varieties because it is used as the medium for education in England. This role of Standard English encourages some people to regard non-standard speakers as being uneducated and often by a further unwarranted extension as being unintelligent. But students of language should regard all varieties of English as equivalent vehicles of communication, even though within society generally different prejudices and attitudes may be attached to particular varieties. Because of the position of Standard English it is often taken subconsciously as a norm in discussions of language acquisition, change and varieties. Thus discussions of past forms of English are based on a comparison between that form and modern Standard English. Similarly, in discussions of language acquisition, it may be assumed that a child is moving towards the acquisition of the elements of Standard English rather than of another variety. Discussions of language varieties will frequently involve comparisons between a given variety and Standard English. Because of the limits on the size of this book, we follow this general procedure here. But in discussions of language and the social context we look at attitudes towards different varieties of English, and this means knowing something about those varieties and about the structure of society. Whereas Chapters 2 and 3 often compare one variety of language with the standard, Chapter 4 on Language Variety and the Social Context matches linguistic performance to social structure and is consequently of a rather different nature.

Language study, however, is more than simply understanding how the elements within a sentence are made up and ordered. Sentences have to be joined together to produce a text, whether written or spoken, in order to put across a point of view, persuade someone else to do what you want, or for whatever purpose the text is intended. Language is used for communication. It is addressed to a specific audience and therefore falls into a particular type or genre. An obituary is a different genre from a romantic novel, and a writer will adjust his or her English to meet what he or she considers the requirement of each. Hence in Chapter 5 we look at English beyond the sentence, at English as discourse directed towards particular communicative goals. To have a good command of English it is not sufficient to know the parts of a sentence, and equally to study English language fully one needs to look at the choices one makes to achieve one's communicative ends. *Gormless* and *stupid* may mean the same thing, but we would use them on different occasions according to who our audience was, where we were speaking, and what effect we were trying to achieve. To study how others have adapted their language to particular genres and goals should enable you to use your own language in similar ways.

One of the exciting aspects of language study is that since language is all around us, anyone can study it. Does your father use different language from your mother? Do you use language to irritate or exclude your parents? If you do, what language do you use, and why? Chapter 6 looks at ways in which you can organise language research, for the best way to find out how language works is to conduct your own research. But it is necessary to have some framework in which to carry out your investigation: how to decide on a project, how to collect data, how to interpret it, and how to set out your results.

It has been said that language is power, and a knowledge of how language works may well increase your self-confidence in using it. But studying language is fun because of the uses to which it is put and it is important because language will be with you and surround you all your life. Enjoy it.

1

Describing the Structure and Sounds of English

INTRODUCTION

In all areas of language study we need to be able to describe the language used by identifying the elements in a given utterance, and the way they fit together. This is what we mean by grammar. A sound understanding of grammar and its terminology is the language student's best tool. For many students, the word 'grammar' has unpleasant associations; it reminds us of the tricky bits which often took a long time to master when we were learning French or German or Latin. But for those of us whose mother-tongue is English, learning about the structure of English should present few difficulties as we have been learning and practising it since we first began to acquire language in our first year of life. We have been experts for years.

Two things obscure our perception of our expertise. The first is that we lack the terms necessary for describing the language; the second arises from the historical association of grammar and correctness.

• As we saw in the Introduction, there is more than one variety of English, and each variety has a structure which is correct for that variety. Historically, however, grammar was not just a way of describing the language; it was also regarded as a set of rules according to which English ought to be organised. These rules referred to the standard written form of English. They took no account of spoken language, regional varieties, levels of formality or the fact that language is constantly changing. (These matters are discussed in subsequent chapters.) Because spoken, regional, informal, and more modern varieties of English frequently differ from the written standard they were (and are) considered 'incorrect' by those who favoured the use and teaching of the rules of written

Standard English. Modern linguistics, on the other hand, is founded on the principle that language should be suitable for its purpose and, as purposes vary, non-standard forms may be not only suitable but correct in certain contexts.

• These two attitudes need not be mutually exclusive. Very few people speak according to the rules of written Standard English; each regional variety has its own grammatical rules; informal language can often be recognised by its differences from Standard English; and the changes which are constantly occurring demand that we should from time to time take stock of what does constitute Standard English and adjust the rules accordingly. Equally, however, we must respect Standard English and its conventions; because it is the accepted written form used in education we need to be able to read and write it. Reading Standard English will familiarise us with its rules; a rather more detailed study of its rules is required if we are to express ourselves clearly in written English.

In the first part of this chapter we introduce and explain some of the basic terms for describing English, and discuss some of the simpler structures. The terms are equally suitable for describing non-standard varieties or Standard English, though the examples are all of Standard English.

THE UNITS OF A SENTENCE

The structural units of language with which we are most familiar are the word and the sentence. Other units are the morpheme, which is a smaller unit than the word, and the phrase and the clause which come between the word and the sentence. These units of language which are explained in the following pages can be arranged in an ascending hierarchy: morpheme (p. 3), word (p. 5), phrase (p. 11), clause (p. 15), and sentence (p. 17). Each level or rank in the hierarchy contains one or more than one of the units from the level or rank immediately below it. For example, the sentence

The signalman stopped the express train because a heavy snowfall had blocked the line

contains two clauses:

1 *The signalman stopped the express train*
2 *because a heavy snowfall had blocked the line*

Each of these clauses contains three phrases. In the second clause there are the phrases:

1 *a heavy snowfall*
2 *had blocked*
3 *the line*

Each of these phrases is made up of words, three in the first, and two in each of the second and third phrases. Each of these words consists of one morpheme, except *snowfall* and *blocked* which each contain two.

These structural units can function at a lower level or rank in the hierarchy, and they are then said to be **rankshifted**. For example, in the sentence

The heavy snow which fell in the night blocked the line from Edinburgh

the clause *which fell in the night* is part of the phrase *the heavy snow which fell in the night*. The concept of rankshifting is important for understanding the structure of complex sentences which are discussed later in the chapter.

The way in which morphemes (p. 3) combine into words is known as **morphology**. The way in which structural units relate to each other within sentences is known as **syntax**. Sentences may be linked together to form larger stretches of language known as paragraphs or text, but a sentence has no formal grammatical link to any other unit of language. The relationship between sentences in longer stretches of language is known as **discourse**, and will be discussed in a later chapter.

The morpheme

A morpheme is the smallest unit of language which has an independent function.

• Morphemes are not the same as syllables. For example, the words *possess*, *study* and *danger* all have more than one syllable but only one morpheme (i.e. they are monomorphemic), as the meanings or grammatical structures of these words cannot be broken down or simplified any further. These examples can all be built up by the addition of other morphemes which alter either their grammatical function or their meaning. For example, the base form of the verb *possess* can become the past tense by the addition of the past tense morpheme *-ed*: *possessed*; or a noun by the addition of the noun-forming morpheme *-ion*: *possession*; or its meaning can be changed by prefixing the morpheme *re-*: *repossess*. Similarly, the noun *danger* can become an adjective by the addition of the adjectival morpheme *-ous*: *dangerous*; or a verb by prefixing the verb-forming morpheme *en-*: *endanger*.

• Morphemes can be classified as **free morphemes** or **bound morphemes**. **Free morphemes** are monomorphemic words and they can operate freely in the language; for example, *possess, study, danger, boy*. Bound morphemes must combine with other morphemes; for example, *dis-* (bound morpheme) + *possess* (free morpheme) = *dispossess* (word); *study* (free morpheme) + *-ous* (bound morpheme) = *studious* (word); *boy* (free morpheme) + *-s* (bound morpheme) = *boys* (word).

• **Bound morphemes** are inflectional or derivational. Inflectional morphemes are bound morphemes which are part of the grammatical system. As such, their main function is to indicate the plural and possessive forms of nouns, markers of tense and person in verbs, and markers of degree in adjectives, as we shall see below. In texts from earlier stages of English we are likely to find inflections that we do not come across in present-day texts, and there may be more of them. In Old English, the form of English used until about 1150, inflections were used to show how words in sentences related to each other. The development of English has seen a gradual decline in the number of inflections used. Relationships between words nowadays are mainly signalled by **word order**. However, non-standard varieties of contemporary English may use either a different number or a different distribution of morphemes.

• **Derivational morphemes** are part of the process of word formation. They combine with an existing word to form a new word. The prefixes *in-*, *un-* and *dis-* are bound morphemes which can completely alter the meaning of a word. Compare *insecure, unhappy, disconnect* with *secure, happy* and *connect*. Other derivational morphemes can change a word's class. The bound morpheme *-ness* can change an adjective into a noun: *clever+ness = cleverness*; *-ful* can change a noun into an adjective: *care+ful = careful*; and *-ise* can change an adjective into a verb: *equal+ise = equalise*.

The word

The next level in the grammatical hierarchy is the word. Words are easily recognised, especially in writing, where they are separated by spaces. The words in the English language can be divided into nine classes: nouns, verbs, adjectives, adverbs, pronouns, determiners, prepositions, conjunctions and interjections.

• These classes may be divided into two groups, open classes and closed classes. Open classes have a very large membership and can have more words added to them as the language grows and changes. The open classes are noun, verb, adjective, and adverb. These words have a definable meaning which can be found using a dictionary, and they are also known as lexical words. Pronouns, determiners, prepositions, conjunctions and interjections are all closed classes. Closed classes have a smaller, restricted membership which rarely changes. They have a grammatical meaning and are often referred to as structural or functional words. Many words belong to more than one class. Before we can decide on a word's class we need to consider its **meaning**, its **morphology** and its **syntactic function**.

• A **noun** is a word which names something. Nouns can be categorised according to the kind of thing that is named. The most common distinction is that of proper noun and common noun. A proper noun refers to a specific place or person such as *Winchester* or *John Smith*. A proper noun is written with a capital letter. In English, names of months and days are also regarded as proper nouns. A common noun signifies a more generalised range of things, and can be further classified, according to its meaning, into concrete and abstract nouns. Concrete nouns signify material things; for example, *dog, apple, boy*. Abstract nouns signify non-material things, such as ideas, conditions, and feelings; for example, *science, patience, hope*.

Nouns can also be classified according to their countability. Count nouns signify things which can be counted. They have both a singular and a plural form. Both abstract and concrete nouns can be countable; for example, *hope – hopes; apple – apples*. Non-count nouns refer to an undifferentiated mass and do not have a plural form; for example, *knowledge, foliage*. Countability is independent of whether a noun is abstract or concrete. Some nouns may be either count nouns or non-count nouns, but this usually involves at least a slight change of meaning; for example, *Mother made some* cakes (count noun); *Let them eat* cake (non-count noun); and Language *is a human characteristic* (non-count noun); *I speak only one* language (count noun).

Morphologically, nouns can be marked for plural. The usual plural marker is the bound morpheme *-s*; for example, *I have a* cat, *but three* cats *live next door*. The plural forms of some words, such as *child, foot* and *sheep*, are different for historical reasons, and some foreign words which English has borrowed have retained their original plurals: for example, *index, antenna,* and *phenomenon* have the plurals *indices, antennae* and *phenomena*. Nouns are also marked to show possession. The possessive form of the noun also uses the *-s* morpheme, though the *s* is usually preceded or followed by an apostrophe; for example, *The cat's fur is black. The cats' tails were very long*.

A noun occurs as the headword of a noun phrase (see p. 11). Noun phrases can perform different functions in the sentence. They are found chiefly as subject or object in sentence structure, or as complement in a prepositional phrase.

• A **pronoun** is a word which can be used in place of a noun. Pronouns comprise a closed class of words, but there are several different kinds of pronoun:

personal	I, you, he, she, it, we, they
reflexive	myself, yourself, himself, herself, itself, ourselves, themselves
possessive	mine, yours, his, hers, ours, theirs
relative	who, which, whose, whom
demonstrative	this, that, these, those
interrogative	who?, which?, what?
indefinite	something, everything, nothing, someone, everyone, no-one

Pronouns are complicated by the fact that most pronouns exist in **more than one form**. This is because pronouns have retained to a greater extent than either nouns or adjectives the inflectional system they had in Old English. This is most apparent in the personal pronouns which, besides having different forms to denote person, plurality and gender, also have different forms to indicate syntactic function: a subject case for use when the pronoun is the subject of the sentence, as in *He was driving the car*; a possessive case, *John was driving his car*; and a third case which is used for the object and to follow prepositions, *Mary saw him and waited for him*. The complete set of forms for the personal pronouns is as follows:

	Subject case	Possessive case	Object case	
1st person singular	I	my	me	masculine or feminine
2nd person singular or plural	you	your	you	masculine or feminine
3rd person singular	he	his	him	masculine
	she	her	her	feminine
	it	its	it	neuter
1st person plural	we	our	us	masculine or feminine
3rd person plural	they	their	them	masculine or feminine

Reflexive pronouns are marked for person, and demonstratives for plural. Relative pronouns have a subject case, *who*, a possessive case, *whose*, and an object case, *whom*, though this latter form appears to be falling into disuse except in the most formal written English. The form *which* is used as subject and object when referring to inanimate nouns. Relative pronouns occur in relative clauses.

• A **verb** is a word which signifies an action, as in *walk, sing, fly*, or a state, as in *be*. Verbs have two main sub-classes: lexical verbs and auxiliary verbs. A **lexical** verb is one which functions as a vocabulary item; it has a meaning which can be found from the dictionary. Morphologically, lexical verbs have more forms than any other word class. These forms are

The base form	walk	sing	fly
The infinitive	to walk	to sing	to fly
3rd person singular present tense	walks	sings	flies
Past tense	walked	sang	flew
Present participle	walking	singing	flying
Past participle	walked	sung	flown

Auxiliary verbs are used in conjunction with lexical verbs. Auxiliary verbs fall into two categories: primary auxiliaries, *be, have* and *do*, and the modal auxiliaries, *will, shall, can, would, should, could, may, might* and, *must. Ought, used to, need* and *dare* are also included in this category. Auxiliary verbs form a closed subclass, and their meaning is grammatical. The primary auxiliaries can also be used as lexical verbs.

Whether they are being used as lexical or auxiliary verbs will be plain from the context. For example, in the sentence *The cat has a long tail*, *has* has the meaning *possesses*; it is also being used without the help of any other verb, so it must be a lexical verb. In the sentence *The cat has seen the mouse*, *has* is being used in conjunction with *seen*. The lexical meaning of the verb phrase *has seen* is provided by *seen*, so this must be the lexical verb. *Has* fulfils a grammatical function, setting the action at a point in time and a state of completion, so it is the auxiliary verb. As lexical verbs, *be, have* and *do* have the full range of forms; as auxiliary verbs *be* and *have* have the full range of forms, but *do* does not have the infinitive, present participle or past participle forms. The modal auxiliaries have only one form.

The verb or verb phrase is the verb element in sentence structure. Verbs have a wide grammatical scope which will be discussed in the section on the sentence on pp. 17–19.

• It is difficult to describe an **adjective** adequately in terms of its meaning. *Black, lazy* and *wide* are all adjectives, but it is unsatisfactory to think of them in isolation from nouns. They are more easily defined according to their function; adjectives are usually said to **describe nouns**. They can occur immediately before a noun, as in *the wide road* and *the lazy boy*. However, if more than one adjective is used, and they are linked by *and*, they can be placed after the noun: *The cat, black and sleek, slept in the sunshine*. Also, a verb which implies a state can be placed between an adjective and the noun it is describing: *the road was wide* and *the cat grew fat*.

An adjective can have three forms: the **base** form, *wide*; the **comparative**, which is the base form + the inflectional morpheme *-er*, *wider*; and the **superlative**, which is the base form + the inflectional morpheme *-est*, *widest*. In modern English, only adjectives of one syllable and some two-syllable adjectives, notably those that end in *-y*, form their comparative and superlative in this way. Examples are *cold, colder, coldest*; *happy, happier, happiest*; *clever, cleverer, cleverest*. Other two-syllable adjectives and those with three or more syllables form their comparative and superlative by placing the words *more* and *most* immediately before the base form of the adjective. Examples of this are *careful, more careful, most careful*; *dangerous, more dangerous, most dangerous*. Adjectives can be premodified by intensifiers such as *very* and *rather*, though this is not a defining characteristic as it is shared with the next class of word, the adverb.

● The relationship between **adverbs** and verbs is similar to that between adjectives and nouns. They define the **manner, place** or **time** of an action; for example, *he spoke loudly; she arrived recently*; and *we live here*. Some adverbs are used to intensify adjectives and other adverbs: *He was a rather lazy boy*; and *She spoke quite loudly*. Many adverbs can be formed by adding the derivational morpheme *-ly* to an adjective: *quick – quickly; happy – happily*, though many other adverbs, such as *fast, often* and *soon*, are monomorphemic words. When used alone, adverbs can fill the adverbial position in sentence structure.

● **Determiners** are used in conjunction with nouns, and their function is to limit the reference of the noun. They can **identify** the noun or **quantify** the noun. Words which identify the noun include the articles *a* and *the*, the demonstrative pronouns *this, that, these* and *those*, and the possessive form of the personal pronouns, *my, his*, etc. Words which quantify the noun include *some, any, much* and *no*.

Determiners occur in noun phrases, usually at the beginning. A few words, such as *all* or *half*, are sometimes classed as predeterminers and come before the determiner, as in *all the boys*; others, such as numerals, are sometimes classed as postdeterminers and and come after the determiners, as in *the three girls*. Determiners are part of the premodification structure of the noun phrase, that part which comes before the head.

• A **preposition** is a word which comes before a noun or noun phrase in such a way that the preposition and the noun phrase form a structural unit; for example, *under the table; over the moon; through the window*. The resultant structure is known as a **prepositional phrase**. Prepositional phrases can function as the adverbial element in sentence structure; for example, *the cow jumped over the moon*. They can also form part of the postmodification structure of the noun phrase; for example, *the icing on the cake was pink*.

• **Conjunctions** are words which join stretches of language to each other. There are two kinds of conjunction, co-ordinating conjunctions and subordinating conjunctions. **Co-ordinating** conjunctions join structures which are syntactically equal, as shown in the following examples:

1 *The dog danced but the cat sang.* Here the co-ordinating conjunction *but* joins two finite clauses, *the dog danced* and *the cat sang.*
2 *He bought a pint of milk and some biscuits.* Here, *a pint of milk* and *some biscuits* are noun phrases linked by the co-ordinating conjunction *and.*
3 *He saw her on Wednesday or Thursday.* Here, *Wednesday* and *Thursday* are nouns linked by the co-ordinating conjunction *or.*

Subordinating conjunctions link unequal clauses, making one part of the other. Subordinating conjunctions include *if, because, as, while.* In the example, *We will walk if the weather is fine,* there is a clause *if the weather is fine,* but it is part of the whole sentence and cannot stand on its own. The main clause in this sentence, *we will walk* can stand alone. A subordinating conjunction occurs at the beginning of a subordinate clause. The function of conjunctions will become clearer in our discussion of the sentence on pp. 17–19.

• **Interjections** are words which are used to express emotion. Examples are *Oh! Ah! Gosh!* They are usually syntactically independent, and are often separated from the rest of the sentence by an exclamation mark. Although they are regarded as a closed class the membership of the class changes historically. For example, *Crikey!* and *Blimey!* have been displaced by *Damn!* and *Shit!*

The phrase

The next unit in the language hierarchy is the phrase. A phrase is a group of words which have a grammatical relationship to each other and which together form a structural unit. A phrase operates as an element in clause structure.

There are different kinds of phrases, and they are designated according to the class of the most important word they contain, which may be a noun, verb, preposition, adjective or adverb.

• **Adjectival** and **adverbial phrases** are easily recognised, as they usually consist simply of the adjective or adverb preceded by one or more intensifiers. For example, in the sentence *Tomorrow will be very much warmer*, *very much warmer* is the adjectival phrase; the headword is the adjective *warmer* which is intensified by *very much*. Similarly, in the sentence *Yesterday he was received rather less enthusiastically*, *rather less enthusiastically* is an adverbial phrase in which the headword *enthusiastically* is intensified by *rather less*.

• **A noun phrase** is a group of words in which the most important word is a noun or a pronoun. A noun phrase may consist of one word or several words. Where the noun phrase consists of several words the structure can be quite complex. The words which come before the headword are said to premodify the noun, and those which come after to postmodify it. For example, *the big black dog at the gate* is a noun phrase; *dog* is the headword, and it is premodified by *the big black*, and postmodified by *at the gate*.

The structure of a noun phrase before the head most often consists of a determiner and one or more adjectives, as in the example given in the last paragraph, but it can also include words such as *all* or *both* which come before the determiner, and nouns which are being used descriptively. For example, in the noun phrase *both my old school friends*, *friends* is the headword, premodified by the adjective *old* and the noun *school*; the determiner *my* is preceded by *both*. The noun phrase *all the latest garden furniture* has the same structure.

The postmodifier of a noun phrase can be a prepositional phrase, as in *the dog at the gate*, or a non-finite clause, as in *the dog standing at the gate*, or a finite clause, as in *the dog which is standing at the gate*. These structures are discussed below.

• A **prepositional phrase** is a unit of structure in which a preposition is the most important word. The phrase usually consists of a preposition and a noun phrase which is known as the prepositional complement. For example, *at the gate* is a prepositional phrase in which *at* is the preposition and the noun phrase *the gate* is the prepositional complement. As we saw earlier, prepositional phrases can act as adverbials in sentence structure, or they can be post-modifiers in a noun phrase. A non-finite clause consists of a non-finite part of the verb, e.g. *standing*, which usually describes the noun it postmodifies and may be followed by a prepositional phrase, an adverb or an object. A finite clause is a sentence which has been rankshifted to act as a postmodifier and which is usually introduced by a relative pronoun such as *who* or *which*.

• A **verb phrase** is a group of words in which the most important word is a lexical verb. The different forms and combinations of lexical and auxiliary verbs are used to express its many properties and wide grammatical scope. Structurally the verb phrase may consist of one or more verbs. If there is only one verb it must be a lexical verb. For example, in the sentence *Mary opened the letter* the verb phrase *opened* consists of a single lexical verb. Any other verbs in the verb phrase will be primary or modal auxiliaries. A verb phrase may contain several primary auxiliaries, but it can have only one modal auxiliary. If a modal auxiliary is present it is always the first element of the verb phrase; the final element is always a lexical verb. In the sentence *Mary might have been opening the letter*, the verb phrase *might have been opening* contains the modal auxiliary *might* as the first element, followed by two primary auxiliaries *have* and *been*, with the lexical verb *opening* as the final element.

The composition of the verb phrase can indicate one or more of the following properties: tense, finiteness, modality, aspect, voice.

⋆ **Tense** is traditionally regarded as the reference made by the verb to the time when an action occurs. In English only the simple present and the simple past are marked morphologically, as in *sings* and *sang*, and most of the present tense is indicated by the base form of the verb, *sing*. But the relationship between time and tense is more complex. For example, in the sentence *He arrives tomorrow* the verb form indicates present tense but the time of the action is future, as the adverb *tomorrow* makes plain. The simple present and the simple past tenses are indicated by the relevant form of the lexical verb. Compound tenses are those formed by combinations of lexical and auxiliary verbs, though most of these combinations indicate more than tense alone, as is discussed below.

★ A verb is **finite** when it is linked grammatically to a subject, which is the person or thing responsible for the action which the verb signifies. In the sentence *The cat slept* the verb *slept* is finite because it has a grammatical subject, *the cat*. Lexical verbs have finite and non-finite forms. The finite forms are those which indicate the simple present and simple past tenses. The non-finite forms are the infinitive and the present and past participles. Note that the base form of a verb (e.g. *sing*) can function as a finite or non-finite form according to the structure of the verb phrase in which it is used; the past participle of a regular verb usually has the same form as the past tense.

If a verb phrase is finite, the finiteness is always indicated in the **first element**. Modal auxiliaries are always finite, and primary auxiliaries are finite when they are the first element of the verb phrase. Second and subsequent elements of the verb phrase are always non-finite forms. For example, *Mary* opened *the letter* (finite lexical verb); *Mary* was opening *the letter* (finite primary auxiliary, non-finite lexical verb); *Mary* must have been opening *the letter* (finite modal auxiliary, two non-finite primary auxiliaries, non-finite lexical verb).

★ **Modal auxiliaries** do not themselves have lexical meaning, but their presence in the verb phrase modifies the meaning of the lexical verb by including in the meaning such features as possibility (*Mary might open the letter*), intention (*Mary will open the letter*), and obligation (*Mary must open the letter*). The modals *will* and *shall* are often used in verb phrases with a future reference, but they also can express willingness and intention, as in *I'll tell you a story* and *I'll meet you in the library*.

★ **Aspect** is the distinction signalled by the verb phrase between actions which are in progress and actions which are complete. **Progressive aspect** refers to actions which are in progress, and it is indicated by the auxiliary verb *be* and the present participle of the lexical verb. Progressive aspect can occur in the present tense or in the past tense. For example, *Mary is opening the letter* (present progressive); *Mary was opening the letter* (past progressive). Perfective aspect refers to actions which are complete, and is indicated by the auxiliary *have* and the past participle of the lexical verb. It can occur in the present tense or in the past tense. For example, *Mary has opened the letter* (present perfective); *Mary had opened the letter* (past perfective). Aspect is not a feature of those verb phrases which consist of a simple present tense or a simple past tense.

Some verbs do not, under normal circumstances, occur in the progressive form. These are verbs which refer to **states** rather than actions. The sentence *He was seeming happy* is most improbable. Verbs which do not occur in the progressive form are known as **stative** verbs, whereas those which do have a progressive form are known as **dynamic** verbs, and it is these verbs which refer to actions. However, it is possible in certain circumstances to use a progressive form of a stative verb, and it is a feature of style which should not be overlooked.

★ **Voice** refers to the traditional distinction between active and passive voices. The active voice is the more usual form and is found in verb phrases where the grammatical subject is the person or thing responsible for the action. In the sentence *The cat drank the milk*, the grammatical subject *the cat* is the perpetrator of the action. In the sentence *The milk was drunk by the cat* the grammatical subject *the milk* is clearly not the perpetrator of the action but the recipient of it. This sort of construction is known as the passive voice. Passive verb phrases consist of the auxiliary *be* and the past participle of the lexical verb.

• In addition to these properties, the verb phrase can be **positive** or **negative**. Positive verb phrases are unmarked, and negative verb phrases include *not* or its abbreviated form *n't*. A negative verb phrase always contains an auxiliary verb, which may be a primary auxiliary or a modal, and the negative word comes immediately after the first auxiliary, as in *Mary has not opened the letter* and *Mary could not have opened the letter*. If the verb phrase is not marked for modality or aspect the auxiliary verb *do* must be used: *Mary did not open the letter*.

The clause

The clause is the level of language which comes between the phrase and the sentence. It usually contains more than one element of structure but it **must always contain a verb**. The other elements which a clause may contain are subject, one or more objects and adverbials. The particular verb which is being used determines which of these clause elements must be present.

If the verb is finite, the clause will have a subject and will be a finite clause. Examples of finite clauses are:

1   *The cat slept.*
2   *Mary was opening the letter.*

1 contains a finite form of a lexical verb, *slept*.
2 contains a finite form of a primary auxiliary, *was*, linked to a non-finite form of a lexical verb, *opening*.

• The **subject** is most often a noun phrase, though several other structures can fill this slot in the clause. The subject usually precedes the verb.

• **Adverbials** are usually optional elements of clause structure, though with a small number of verbs an adverb of place is essential. Adverbials can be simple adverbs, or other units of structure which function as adverbs. For example, the adverb *here* in the clause *John lives here* could be replaced by the prepositional phrase *in this house*. Since all verbs can be modified by adverbs, adverbials are frequently found as clause elements. Also, a clause can contain many separate adverbials, as in *The athlete ran rapidly round the park for an hour every morning*. Here the adverbials are *rapidly*, a simple adverb; *round the park* and *for an hour* which are prepositional phrases; and *every morning* which is a noun phrase. Adverbials have a less rigid position in the clause than other elements. We could just as easily say *Every morning for an hour the athlete ran rapidly round the park*, or *For an hour every morning the athlete ran rapidly round the park*.

• Other elements in clause structure depend on what the **verb needs** to make it **grammatically complete**. Consider these clauses:

1   *The dog barked*
2   *The children picked*
3   *They gave*
4   *The dog is*

⋆ **1** makes sense as it stands. It would be possible to add a word or phrase as an adverbial, such as *loudly* or *in the night*, but such an element is not necessary for the verb to be grammatically complete. Verbs of this sort are known as **intransitive** verbs. *Arrive, bark* and *cry* are all intransitive verbs. Each of the clauses *The postman arrived, the dog barked,* and *the baby cried* is complete in itself. None of the other examples are considered to be complete sentences as they are given here. For **2** to be complete we need to know what it was that the children picked. Verbs of this sort are known as **transitive** verbs, and they need an object to make them grammatically complete. The object is the person or thing which receives or suffers the action of the verb. In this example we could say *The children picked blackberries.* Some verbs like *give* in **3** are often found with two objects. We could say *They gave the blackberries,* but the clause may still seem incomplete as we expect the blackberries to be given to something or somebody. We could say *They gave the blackberries to the dog,* and in this case both *the blackberries* and *the dog* are objects. In traditional grammar these two objects would be distinguished, with *the blackberries* being the **direct object** and *the dog* the **indirect object**. If the indirect object takes the form of a prepositional phrase, the direct object will come first, as in the last example. However, when this preposition is omitted it is equally acceptable to say *They gave the dog the blackberries.*

⋆ Some verbs are always transitive: *The children picked blackberries; The best man made a speech; Arthur cut his finger.* Some verbs are always intransitive: *The postman arrived; the dog barked; the baby cried.* Many verbs can be used transitively or intransitively: *After tea John played and Anna read* (intransitive); *After tea John played the piano and Anna read her book* (transitive). The object element of the clause is most often a noun phrase, but several other structures can also fill this slot in clause structure. In normal syntax the object usually comes after the verb.

⋆ The objects in **2** and **3** refer to something other than the subject of the verb, but **4** is rather different. **4** is incomplete, and it can be completed in several different ways. One way would be to use an adverbial such as *outside* or *in his basket*. We can also complete the clause by using either a noun or an adjective, but in either case the word used refers to the subject of the verb. For example, we can say *The dog is a mongrel* (noun), or *The dog is sick* (adjective); but in each case we are referring back to the dog, and not to something else. A noun or an adjective used in this way is known as the **complement**.

The sentence

The **sentence** is the highest grammatical level in the grammatical hierarchy. Sentences can be defined in several different ways. From its punctuation we can say it begins with a capital letter and ends with a full stop. Within these limits it must contain one or more clauses. A simple sentence consists of one finite clause made up of the clause elements subject(**S**), verb(**V**), and/or object(s)(**O**), and/or adverbial(s)(**A**), such as *The boy*(**S**) *read*(**V**) *his essay*(**O**) *brilliantly*(**A**). But grammatical completeness on its own is not enough. An utterance such as *The table drove the wisdom succulently* satisfies the grammatical criteria, but it does not make sense. That it should make sense is another essential feature of a sentence.

• Sentences can be classified according to their **structure** or their **function**. Structurally, there are three kinds of sentence which are known as simple, compound and complex sentences.

★ A **simple sentence** is the sort we have already mentioned, which consists of one finite clause only, such as *The cat slept*, or *Mary opened the letter*. These examples are very short. They could be much longer and still be simple sentences; for example, *The tortoiseshell cat lying in her basket with her three kittens had slept peacefully since lunchtime*. The length of this sentence has been achieved by extending the noun phrase which forms the subject, and by adding the two adverbials *peacefully* and *since lunchtime*. It is still a simple sentence because there is only one finite verb phrase. 'Simple' is a grammatical description and does not refer to length or to the amount of information a sentence contains.

★ A **compound sentence** consists of one or more finite clauses which are linked together by co-ordinating conjunctions; for example, *The cat slept and the children played*, and *John played the piano but Anna read her book*. If a compound sentence contains more than two finite clauses they may be put together like a list, and a conjunction used only between the last two, as in *The postman arrived, the dog barked and the baby cried*.

★ A **complex sentence** contains two or more finite clauses, but they are linked together in such a way that one of the clauses is an integral part of the other. This is because the two clauses are linked by a subordinating conjunction. In the sentence *The cat slept while the children played* the clause *while the children played* is the adverbial which tells us when the cat slept. Similarly, in the sentence *The signalman stopped the express train because a heavy snowfall had blocked the line*, the clause *because a heavy snowfall had blocked the line* is an adverbial which tells us why the signalman stopped the train. In each of these examples the first clause is the main clause, and the second is the **subordinate** or **dependent** clause.

★ Subordinate clauses are not always adverbials. In the sentence *The heavy snow which fell in the night blocked the line from Edinburgh*, the clause *which fell in the night* is again a finite clause. This time, the function of this finite clause is to postmodify the noun *snow* in the noun phrase which forms the subject of the sentence.

Subordinate clauses can also function as the subject, object or complement of a sentence, as in the following examples:

Subject	*That he won the marathon surprised everyone*
Object	*We wondered if it would rain*
Complement	*The result was that England won.*

• Sentences can be classified according to their function as statements, questions, commands or exclamations. These sentence types are marked syntactically.

★ A **statement** or declarative sentence is an informative sentence in which the subject usually precedes the verb; for example, *Mary opened the letter straightaway*. The order of elements in this sentence is **SVOA**. As we showed earlier, the adverbial position is quite flexible. The order of other elements can be altered for stylistic reasons, as in *The letter she read at once*, which has the order OSVA.

★ A **question**, or interrogative sentence, asks for information. The verb phrase in a question must always contain one or more auxiliary verbs, and the subject comes after the first auxiliary verb; for example, *Has Mary opened the letter?*, *Could Mary have opened the letter?*

⋆ A **command** or imperative sentence is a sentence which issues an order. The verb is often described as being in the imperative mood. In Modern English the imperative consists simply of the base form of the verb. It is recognisable as the imperative because the sentence does not have a grammatical subject so that the verb phrase is the first element of the sentence; for example, *Open the letter.*

⋆ **Exclamations** are sentences which express emotion. They usually begin with *what* or *how*, words which are more typically used for asking questions. In exclamations the subject comes before the verb, but is itself preceded by the object or complement. Examples of exclamations are *How hot it is!* and *What big eyes you have!* Exclamations are frequently not grammatical sentences. They may be single words such as *Damn!* or *Hell!* or they may be phrases such as *My goodness!* or *What a mess!* or *How lovely!* In all these cases the utterance is punctuated as though it were a sentence, beginning with a capital letter and ending with an exclamation mark which has the same force as a full stop.

• Stretches of language which are punctuated as sentences but in which an obligatory element such as subject or verb is missing are known as **minor sentences**. Such sentences can be used deliberately to produce particular effects. They are frequently found in advertising copy and emotional descriptions where their use suggests more than they actually say. For example, a holiday brochure might include a 'sentence' such as *Miles and miles of golden sands*, where the noun phrase on its own is sufficient to produce a response in the reader.

THE SOUNDS OF ENGLISH

One aspect of English which we have not mentioned so far is the **phonology** or system of sounds which comprises the English language. Phonology is not part of grammar, but it is so fundamental to the study of language that it is appropriate to include it here.

Earlier we discussed the morpheme as a unit of word structure. Words can also be broken down into their constituent sounds. The

smallest unit of sound which can bring about a change of meaning is
called a **phoneme**.

- English has 44 phonemes, made up of 24 consonants and 20 vowel
sounds. A **consonant** is a sound made when the airflow through the
mouth is either completely blocked momentarily or very severely
restricted; a **vowel** is a sound produced without such restrictions in
the airflow. The vowel sounds can be further divided into 12 'pure'
vowel sounds and 8 diphthongs, or sounds which glide between
two vowel sounds.

- As there are more phonemes than letters of the alphabet, a special
system of notation known as the **phonetic alphabet** has been
developed to distinguish phonemes in writing. The phonemes of
English are represented in the phonetic alphabet in the following
way.

Consonants

/p/	as in *p*in
/b/	as in *b*in
/t/	as in *t*en
/d/	as in *d*en
/k/	as in *c*ave
/g/	as in *g*ave
/s/	as in *s*ip
/z/	as in *z*ip
/f/	as in *f*an
/v/	as in *v*an
/θ/	as in *th*in
/ð/	as in *th*is
/ʃ/	as in *sh*in
/ʒ/	as in bei*g*e
/tʃ/	as in *ch*eap
/dʒ/	as in *j*eep
/m/	as in *m*et
/n/	as in *n*et
/ŋ/	as in ba*ng*
/h/	as in *h*ut

/w/	as in *w*it
/j/	as in *y*et
/r/	as in *r*at
/l/	as in *l*ot

Vowels

/æ/	as in b*a*t
/ɑ/	as in b*a*r
/i/	as in b*ea*t
/ɪ/	as in b*i*t
/e/	as in b*e*d
/ɒ/	as in p*o*t
/ɔ/	as in p*o*rt
/ʊ/	as in p*u*t
/u/	as in b*oo*t
/ʌ/	as in b*u*t
/ɜ/	as in b*i*rd
/ə/	as in *a*bout

Diphthongs

/eɪ/	as in b*ay*
/aɪ/	as in b*uy*
/ɔɪ/	as in b*oy*
/aʊ/	as in p*out*
/əʊ/	as in b*oat*
/ɪə/	as in b*eer*
/ɛə/	as in b*are*
/ʊə/	as in b*oor*

The symbols in this list are taken from the International Phonetic Alphabet (IPA), a system of notation which provides a symbol for every linguistic sound so that, in theory, all the languages of the world can be transcribed.

• Speech sounds are made by varying the way in which air passes through the mouth and nasal cavity. The organs which are involved are shown in Figure 1.1.

Figure 1.1   The organs of speech

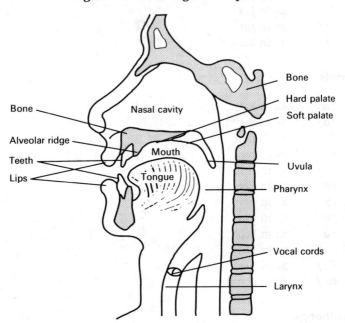

★ Consonant sounds are described in terms of which speech organs
   are involved in their production. This is known as **the place of
   articulation**. *Bilabial* sounds involve the lips; *dental*, the teeth and
   the tongue; *labio-dental*, the lower lip and upper teeth; *alveolar*, the
   tongue and the ridge behind the teeth; *palato-alveolar*, the hard
   palate, the alveolar ridge and the tongue; *palatal*, the hard palate
   and the tongue; *velar*, the soft palate and the tongue; *glottal*, the
   vocal cords.
       If, in addition, the vocal cords vibrate, the sound is said to be
   voiced; if the vocal cords do not vibrate, the sound is **voiceless**.

The manner of articulation describes the way the passage of air is
obstructed through the vocal organs. Complete blocking of the air-
stream produces *plosive* consonants; a narrowing of the air-stream
produces *fricatives*. A plosive followed immediately by a fricative
gives an *affricate* consonant. A *nasal* consonant is one in which the air
escapes via the nasal cavity while the mouth is obstructed. A *lateral*

consonant occurs when there is a partial blockage and air escapes round the side of the tongue. A *frictionless continuant* is produced by reducing the airflow but not enough to cause friction.

Table 1.1 (on p. 24) shows how the consonants of British English can be described. For example, /w/ is a bilabial frictionless continuant; /z/ is a voiced alveolar fricative; and /k/ is a voiceless velar plosive. If you practise making the different sounds whilst carefully noting the position of your tongue, you will soon become familiar with the meaning of these terms.

★ There is no obstruction of airflow in the production of **vowel sounds**. Different sounds are produced by changing the shape of the space inside the mouth, primarily by altering the position of the tongue. The three main points to consider when describing vowel sounds are the closeness of the tongue to the roof of the mouth; the part of the tongue which is highest; and the position of the lips. If the tongue is high or 'close' the mouth will not be open very much; if the tongue is low or 'open', the mouth will also be open.

The position of the tongue for the production of the vowels of British English (RP) is shown in Figure 1.2.

Figure 1.2   Table showing place of articulation of English vowels

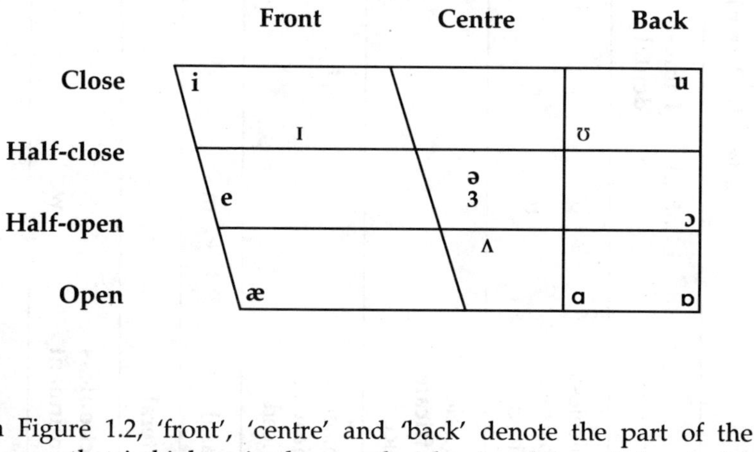

In Figure 1.2, 'front', 'centre' and 'back' denote the part of the tongue that is highest in the mouth; 'close' and 'open' denote the closeness of the tongue to the roof of the mouth.

Table 1.1 The place of articulation of English Consonants

	Bilabial	Labio-dental	Dental	Alveolar	Palato-Alveolar	Palatal	Velar	Glottal
Voiceless **Plosive** voiced	p b			t d			k g	
Voiceless **Affricate** voiced					tʃ dʒ			
Voiceless **Fricative** voiced		f v	θ ð	s z	ʃ ʒ			h
Nasal	m			n			ŋ	
Lateral				l				
Fictionless continuant	w			r		j		

From Figure 1.2 we can see that the phoneme /i/ is made with the front of the tongue raised close to the hard palate and the lips spread. /u/ is made with the back of the tongue raised close to the hard palate and the lips rounded. /ɔ/ is made with the back of the tongue raised, but not very high, and the lips rounded. If you practise making the vowel sounds in order, from close to open, front to back, open to close, you will feel the changing positions of your tongue.

The remaining vowel sounds, the **diphthongs**, can also be demonstrated diagramatically. During the production of a diphthong the sound glides from one vowel towards another. This is done by changing the position of the tongue. Diphthongs are classed as closing diphthongs or centring diphthongs, according to the direction of the glide. The direction of the glide is shown by the arrows in Figure 1.3.

Figure 1.3   Table showing place of articulation of diphthongs

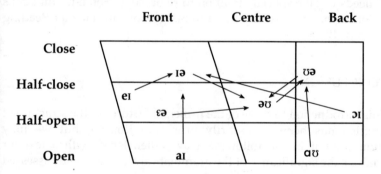

• We should also be aware of the **prosodic features** of the language. These are phonological features which extend over more than just one sound in an utterance. They include rhythm, and patterns of intonation.

★ English is a stress-timed language, which means that stressed syllables occur at more or less regular intervals. The stress pattern can sometimes indicate a word's class, for example 'conduct' can be pronounced /ˈkɒndəkt/, a noun, or /kənˈdʌkt/, a verb. A stressed syllable is marked by placing a high vertical mark before it.

* Intonation is usually discussed in terms of **rising** and **falling** intonation. It is often said that, in English, declarative sentences (statements) are spoken with a falling intonation, and interrogative sentences (questions) with a rising intonation. While it is not possible to make a hard and fast rule about this, it is usually true that questions which have the grammatical form of statements usually have a rising intonation. Try saying, 'He's going to Australia' as a statement, then as a question, and listen carefully to how it is said.
* Ear-training is very important in learning to recognise all phonological features, but prosodic features especially need much practice. Stress and intonation can be combined in different ways to create different meanings or attitudes on the part of the speaker. Try saying 'oh' in different ways to demonstrate this. Other words with a range of possible intonation are 'Yes' and 'Really'.
* Anybody undertaking a project involving spoken language needs to give special attention to phonology. Some useful books for further reading are listed in Suggestions for Further Reading on p. 170.

CONCLUSION

This introduction to some of the principal features of the structure of English has been necessarily brief and limited, but we may summarise it in the following way. When faced with a text for analysis the significance of the grammatical features can be assessed by considering the following points:

1 Is there anything **unusual** about the word classes, such as a word from one class being given a different function?
2 Are sentences **simple, compound** or **complex**?
3 Do sentences express a **statement**, a **question** or a **command**?
4 What is the **structure** of the clauses?
5 What structures comprise the **clause elements**?
6 What is the structure of the **noun phrases**?
7 What can we say about the **verb phrases**? Are the verbs lexical or auxiliary (primary or modal); finite or non-finite;

present or past; progressive or perfective; transitive or intransitive; active or passive; positive or negative; stative or dynamic?

Although the written English we have discussed in this chapter is the standard variety, the advantages of being able to discuss the grammatical features of all varieties of English in this way should become more apparent as you read further in this book and consider the nature of various sorts of non-standard language.

Spoken language in particular may present some difficulties because the sentence as a unit of organisation is not always clearly defined in speech. The following is a transcription of part of a spoken description of 'The foundry', a former industrial premises that has been converted into a training centre for climbers.

> it's an indoor climbing wall it's an old works they've knocked all the floors out and over the brickwork they've concreted and er they've put a whole lot of climbing walls up that have little bolt-on holds various different shapes one or two or three fingers or jugholds or all sorts of things and you can change them round if you change the holds so you can always keep changing the wall . . .

In this text it is possible to identify **five sentences**, especially if you hear the speech and take account of the intonation patterns. The sentences are:

1 it's an indoor climbing wall
2 it's an old works
3 they've knocked all the floors out and over the brickwork they've concreted
4 [and er] they've put a whole lot of climbing walls up that have little bolt-on holds various different shapes one or two or three fingers or jugholds or all sorts of things
5 [and] you can change them round if you change the holds so you can always keep changing the wall . . .

• **1** and **2** are simple sentences, each with the structure subject verb complement (**SVC**), with *it* as the subject, an abbreviated form of *is* for the verb and a noun phrase for the complement.

• **3** is a compound sentence, with two finite clauses linked by *and*. The first clause has the structure (**S**) *they* (**V**) *'ve knocked* (**O**) *all the walls* (**A**) *out*, and the second (**A**) *over the walls* (**S**) *they* (**V**) *'ve concreted*.

• **4** has the structure **SVOA**. The subject is *they* and the verb is *'ve put*. The adverbial *up* is embedded in the object which takes up all the rest of the sentence. Structurally, the object is a noun phrase. The headword *wall* is premodified by *climbing*, and the phrasal quantifier *a whole lot of*. The adverbial *up* comes next, and what follows is a relative clause postmodifying *walls*. In this relative clause the subject is *that* and the verb is *have*. The object is a complex noun phrase in which the headword *holds* is premodified by the adjectives *little* and *bolt-on* and postmodified by another complex noun phrase which comprises the rest of the sentence. In this noun phrase the headword *shapes* is premodified by *various* and *different* and postmodified by three co-ordinate noun phrases, *one or two or three fingers, jugholds, all sorts of things*. These three noun phrases are joined by the co-ordinating conjunction *or*.

• Try analysing **5** yourself. In any particular linguistic or stylistic analysis some grammatical features will be more significant than others, but we must recognise them all if we are to describe any text accurately.

2

Language Acquisition

INTRODUCTION

In this chapter we discuss some of the stages and processes involved in the acquisition of language by a child. We are concerned here with children in a homogeneous linguistic environment, i.e. with parents and other relatives who all use a single language in their day-to-day communication, and with children who develop normally in so far as they have no physical or mental impediment which might hinder their acquisition of language. We shall naturally be focussing on English as the language which is acquired, though occasional reference to studies involving other languages may be made. Scholarly interest in the acquisition of language is relatively recent, though it has important implications for theories of language as well as for education and socio- and psycholinguistics.

At this stage it is important that we issue a general caveat. In what follows we refer to stages of development in a child's language acquisition and we have to give approximate ages at which each stage may be reached. It must be emphasised that the ages given are approximate and that every child will differ in some respect. In giving an average age, it follows that some children are quicker than the average and others slower. The speed at which an individual child acquires language should not be related to his or her intellectual potential; such an extrapolation would be quite unwarranted.

In referring to the age of a child there is a convention that the year comes first followed by a semi-colon which is then followed by the month, so that 3;2 means three years and two months old and 0;10 means ten months old. If days in the month are needed they are added in brackets so that 1;3(5) means one year, three months and five days.

In describing language acquisition it is possible to take each chronological stage in a child's development separately or to take each feature of language separately and to trace it chronologically. In what follows we will generally follow the latter pattern.

PRE-SPEECH DEVELOPMENTS

Although a child produces what may be recognised as meaningful utterances in a given language from the age of about one year, this does not mean that no linguistic developments have taken place before then. Even when in the womb a child may be able to distinguish sounds since the organs of the ear appear to be formed about five months after conception. It is possible, for example, that a baby learns the rhythms of its mother's speech while still in the womb.

After birth and in the first year of life a baby listens to a great deal of language, some of which is directed to it personally and the rest of which takes place in its environment. The baby itself also makes sounds which progress from cooing and laughing to random vocalisation and babbling. In the period 0;6 to 0;9 of its development a baby starts to emit rhythmical sounds and it has been shown that these sounds differ according to the language environment in which the baby finds itself. At this stage, the baby could be said to be tuned into the language which it will later learn. It is presumably largely from its own reception and perception of language that it can develop this skill. It recognises individual voices and it picks up the rhythms of those voices which it is able to replicate in its own way. This emphasises the importance of speaking to a child under one year, a task which might at first seem rather unproductive since a child cannot reply; a mother appears to take part in a one-sided exchange. But not only does the child begin to get a feel for the language through its rhythm, it also begins to enter into the social bonding through its mother and her language with the world around it.

Towards the end of its first year a child may start to make sounds which could almost be said to have symbolic meaning and certainly are so interpreted by many parents. Although such sounds may have no phonetic relationship to the adult language, they may approximate to words if they fulfil the following criteria. They should be isolable units; they should recur at frequent intervals; they should be uttered in particular social contexts; and they should exhibit some embryonic phonemic structure. Some reporters have noted that children may at this age utter a particular sound such as /ɑ/ to indicate pleasure and another such as /ɪ/ to indicate rejection. Although it is difficult to be certain about the interpretation of such sounds, it seems quite reasonable to suppose that such a stage in a child's linguistic development does indeed take place.

SOUNDS

It is during the first year that a baby starts to make sounds which can be understood as recognisable sounds in a language rather than as simple noises like cooing. At this stage, a baby is able to produce a sequence of sounds consisting of two sounds in the consonant–vowel (**CV**) order to give forms like *ma* and *da*. It is unlikely that a baby will produce a **VC** or **CC** sequence. A baby will produce a sequence like *ma* rather than one like *am*, and consonant clusters like *sp* or *tr* are most unlikely to occur. The **CV** sequence may well appear early because it approximates most closely to cooing. It then becomes possible for the baby to repeat these sounds to provide a series like *mamama*, which many mothers can easily interpret as signifying that their child is trying to say the baby form of *Mummy*, though such an interpretation seems improbable. It is likely that babies at this stage cannot yet distinguish sounds very well and they have a simple repertoire of those sounds which they find easiest to produce physiologically. It is difficult to predict which sounds might appear first in a baby's speech, but some studies suggest that they are most likely to start with consonants made with the lips (bilabial) and these include /**m, b, p**/. At the same time in view of what has been written above it is not surprising that children find it easier to pronounce consonants at the beginning of a syllable rather than at its end. The ability to pronounce a sequence like *da* does not guarantee that a child could also say *dad* with the same consonant at the end of the syllable. A child may well find it easier to add further consonants to its repertoire at the beginning of syllables before it begins to produce consonants at their end. The consonants which are most likely to appear first at the end of syllables are the fricatives /**f, s**/, probably because they can be protracted in pronunciation and because /**f**/ in particular is not too far removed from some of the babbling sounds it makes. After tackling the bilabial consonants at the beginning of syllables a child may well add the sounds /**d, f, g, h, k, n**/ in initial position.

Substitution

A feature of the speech of young children is substitution, when a sound which they find difficult to make is replaced by another sound which they find easier to produce. Five types of substitution have been recorded by researchers.

• The first is where a fricative such as /f/ is replaced by a plosive such as /p, b, t, d/. This does not mean that all fricatives are replaced by plosives in a child's speech, but only that there is a tendency for children to do this. It is not easy to predict when this substitution will occur or how often. But many children will say /ti/ for *sea* and /pɪ/ for *fish*, in which the final consonant has been lost as well. In this as in the other general cases of substitution examples can be found from many other languages as well as from English.

• The second is where sounds which are made further back in the mouth such as velar and palatal consonants are replaced by sounds which are made further forward in the mouth. Thus /k, g/ which are velar consonants may be replaced by /t/, an alveolar consonant, and /ʃ/ which is a palato-alveolar consonant may be replaced by /z/ which is alveolar. Thus *goose* and *call* may be pronounced /dus/ and /tɑ/ and *shoe* may occur as /zu/.

• The third category is the substitution of the liquid sounds /l, r/ by glide sounds /w, j/, again because a child finds the latter sounds easier to produce. Examples include /wedi/ for *ready* and /jek/ for *leg*. This process appears to be commoner in English than some other languages, for a language such as French does not use the glide /j/ initially and has a restricted usage of /w/. This form of substitution in English children suggests that they are already adopting English phonological patterns.

• A fourth category is vocalisation, whereby a consonant already acting as a syllable on its own develops further to a vowel by losing its consonatal quality. This process, when for example the final syllable in *bottle* becomes first the syllabic consonant /l̩/ and then a vowel, is particularly common in English which contains a host of these syllabic consonants. It is naturally not found in those languages which make little use of syllabic consonants. Examples include the forms /æpə/ for *apple* and /badɑ/ for *bottom*.

• Finally there is the tendency in young children towards vowel neutralisation, that is the process whereby different vowels are pronounced as one or two vowels especially those which are centralised such as /ɑ, ʌ/. Since children often find it easier to pronounce vowels than consonants, this process is relatively early and may be abandoned quite young by many children. In the last category we saw that *bottom* could be pronounced /badɑ/ with both vowels represented as /ɑ/, and a similar vowel sound can be heard in some children's pronunciation of *hug* as /hɑd/.

Assimilation

Assimilation is the process by which one sound is attracted to a neighbouring sound so that it matches that sound in quality through losing those features which are different in quality.

• Consonants tend to be **voiced** when preceding a vowel, but when they follow a vowel if they survive they are often **unvoiced**. Some sounds which are otherwise identical in place and manner of articulation differ only in whether the vocal cords are close together or apart as the air passes through from the lungs. When they are close together they vibrate and produce a voiced quality. You can hear this yourself if you produce the two sounds /z/ and /s/, the first of which is voiced. Examples of this process in children include *pig* pronounced as /bɪk/, where voiceless initial /p/ has given way to voiced /b/ and voiced final /g/ has given way to voiceless /k/, and /bɪp/ for *bib* and /ek/ for *egg* in which the final consonants are unvoiced. In fact the unvoicing of final consonants is a feature which is found in English throughout its history and is found still in several dialects.

• Consonants tend to **assimilate** so that in a sequence **CVC(V)** the initial and final consonants will tend to assume the same quality if their quality is different in the adult language. Two patterns are common in English children's language which lead to initial and final consonants being both velar or both labial. In /gʌk/ for *duck* and /gʌŋ/ for *tongue*, the initial consonants have become velars to assimilate to the final consonant. In /bʌb/ for *tub* and /babu/ for *table*, the initial consonants have become bilabial to echo the second consonant.

• **Vowel assimilation** is also found, and usually takes the form that unstressed vowels adopt the quality of the stressed vowels, even though the quality of that vowel is itself different from the one in adult language. A child could pronounce the words *flower* and *table* as /fawɑ/ and /dubʊ/, in which the second vowel has the same quality as the first even though it may be short whereas the main vowel is long.

Other features of sound production

We have already noted that babies find it difficult to pronounce consonant clusters and this is carried through to early in the third year by many children, and it is characteristic of most languages. Forms like /pɑ/ and /des/ for *play* and *dress* are common.

Another feature which carries through quite commonly to the beginning of the third year is the fall of final consonants, a feature which is also characteristic of English throughout its history. Before a child learns to say *bib* in an adult way, it may first say /bɪ/ with loss of final consonant and then /bɪp/ with final unvoicing before it arrives at /bɪb/. Other examples already cited include /pɪ/ for *fish* and /kɑ/ for *call*. Deletion of unstressed syllables occurs particularly when the unstressed syllable precedes a stressed one, and although this is most noticeable at the beginning of a word it can also occur within a word. Words like *banana* and *potato* may become /nɑnɑ/ and /dɒdɒ/, and the name *Jennika* (one of the children whose language has been studied) was pronounced by her as /geŋkɑ/. Finally reduplication is a common feature of children's language so that the same **CV** sequence is repeated, usually identically. We have already noted this with /mɑmɑ/ for *Mummy*, similarly *water* can appear as /wɑwɑ/.

It should perhaps be added at this point that many children have a particular predilection for a certain sound and will tend to produce that sound in many words and so fail to go along with some of the general trends mentioned above. A child's preference for a sound or even a few sounds may lead to its speech being quite different from that of its siblings. Most of the tendencies we have noted indicate a simplification of sounds which children make in order to communicate, presumably because they find some sounds and combinations of sounds difficult to utter or because they have not yet learned sufficient discrimination to distinguish sounds and so choose the easy options. Once again we must emphasise that we have outlined some general tendencies of the production of sound by children in their earliest years, say to the age of three, but that each child is different in the sounds it produces and in the speed at which it discards the sounds which differ from those of adult language.

VOCABULARY AND MEANING

Before children start to use words, they undertake actions which many parents think are meaningful. In many cases children seem to have been taught such actions in a manner that resembles the training of animals so that they respond to specific stimuli which are context bound. Although we like to think that the actions the children perform show they understand what they are asked to do, their understanding is often different from what we would like to think it is.

A Russian scholar has reported the case of a child who was taught to turn to the picture of Lenin on a particular wall whenever he was asked the question 'Where is Lenin?'. It was assumed that the child related the word *Lenin* to the photograph and hence understood that this word referred to the man in the photograph. But the photograph was removed from the wall and when the question 'Where is Lenin?' was asked after that, the child still turned to the wall on which the photograph had been placed. It is not clear precisely what the child understood the question 'Where is Lenin?' to mean, but it is clear that the assumption that he understood the word *Lenin* to refer to the man in the photograph is unwarranted.

An American scholar has similarly reported that when she asked her son the question 'Where are the shoes?', he would crawl to the cupboard where her shoes were normally kept as if to find the shoes as a response to the question. But on occasion the mother put her shoes on the carpet outside the cupboard and when she asked her son the same question he would ignore her shoes as he passed them on the way to the cupboard. Evidently the word *shoes* did not have the meaning for him that one might have assumed.

At first children respond to specific stimuli in very specific contexts and it does not follow that they attach any meaning to the sounds which they hear as part of a request or command; or rather, the meaning they attach to them is different from those that adults attach to them. It is easy to overinterpret what a child understands unless experiments are very carefully set up and controlled. Words are abstract and when fully understood can be generated in totally different circumstances and contexts. It takes time for this to happen, but until it does one cannot say that a child understands the word.

Learning and distinguishing meaning

Children first learn words within a specific context and consequently limit the meaning of such words to that context. They will probably pick up some of the associations of that context as part of the meaning of the words. If a child learns the word *car* from model cars which he plays with, he may not make an immediate extension of that word to the cars which are found in the street and which can move without being pushed. Equally if a child learns the meaning of the word *car* by watching moving cars from a window, it may not extend that word to either stationary or toy cars. Particular words may be associated with particular actions. Waving your hand and saying *bye-bye* to daddy as he leaves in the morning may mean that the word is associated closely with the waving action and is not repeated separately from it. Equally the word *bye-bye* may be linked by the child to the departure of its father or mother every morning and not be extended as a general word for leave-taking.

Words are interpreted by children in a different way from that used by adults because the meaning is either restricted or extended. It may be easiest to consider the hierarchical ordering of the meaning of words, which we can do by arranging a tree diagram as in Figure 2.1. In Figure 2.1 all examples of a particular group will belong to the groups above it on the tree, but not all examples of a given group will belong to any group which is underneath it on the tree.

This tree is by no means exhaustive, for it is meant to be illustrative. If you take a group lower down and trace it up through the links, the member of a lower group will also be a member of all the other groups above it. All daddys are male and adult and human and animate. But the reverse is not true because not all adult males are daddys; some may be married and have no children and some may be unmarried and childless. Children will often

Figure 2.1

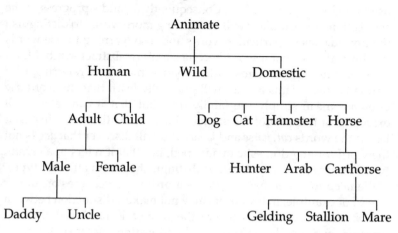

generalise a word in one of the lower groups by assuming that it refers to all members of a higher group. Thus it may assume that *daddy* refers to all adult males or it may assume that *cat* is a word that refers to all domestic animals. Similarly if its parents have a dog called *Rover*, it might assume that all dogs are called *rover*.

Naturally children can extend the meaning of words in other directions because of associations which may not be immediately apparent to adults. A child can pick up the fact that an object is round, such as a clock, and extend its word *tick-tock* to anything which is round, such as a cake or even a face. Or if the family owns a red car, the child may associate the word *car* with redness as much as with the mechanical vehicle which moves. Hence other objects which are red may also come to be called *car*. It is also quite common for children to restrict the meaning of a word to an object with which they are familiar rather than to regard it as the name of a whole group of objects. The word *sock* may be restricted by a child to its own socks rather than to those of any other member of the family, or if its socks are all white, it may restrict the meaning of *sock* to the category of white sock. Individual children can extend the meaning of individual words in ways which are quite puzzling, and a lot of interesting research can be done in this area.

It follows from what has been written that children will use a single word in a variety of meanings which an adult might use different words for. As we have seen the word *tick-tock* might be used for clock, cake and face. Consequently a child's progress in the acquisition of vocabulary will be learning more words to distinguish the **boundaries** of particular words and also learning to use words **symbolically** so that a word becomes a more abstract symbol for a class or category of items rather than a means of referring to a particular item. Thus a child will gradually learn that the word *dog* does not mean simply the family dog, but that it can refer to all examples of this part of the animal kingdom. At the same time as it learns the words *cat, horse* and *hamster*, it will discover that *dog* is not the word for any domestic quadruped, but that it refers to a certain type of quadruped which can be distinguished from all other types.

We need to remember that this is a process which goes on all our lives. For example, many adults may not make a distinction between a *book* and a *manuscript*, where the former is produced through printing and the latter through handwriting, because to many people any writing which occurs in hardcovers is a *book*. Equally they may not distinguish a *paperback* from a *hardback*, because they are both books. Throughout our lives we continue to learn words which divide what had been one category into several sub-categories, often depending upon what our interests and communicative needs are. This is exactly the same with children as they learn their vocabulary.

Types of word learned

It is hardly surprising that children's early vocabulary should be largely made up of words that refer to their **immediate environment**. Since they often also learn from having things pointed out to them or from being told what the correct word is for a particular thing, not unnaturally it is the names of things they acquire first. This also means that their early vocabulary will consist largely of nouns. To this they will then add some verbs and adjectives during their second and third years. Their vocabulary will consist at first of lexical words, those words which are said to carry meaning within themselves, and it is only later that they learn the grammatical words, those words like prepositions and conjunctions which help to organise the lexical words in a grammatical framework to express their relations.

A child's world is immediate and concrete. Important to it are the people it depends on, the food it needs, its own body and bodily functions, and the clothes and toys it possesses. The words it learns first are likely to be concrete nouns referring to these general areas of immediate concern to it. *Mummy* and *Daddy* and the words for other relatives such as grandparents and for siblings are naturally among its first words, even though they appear in phonological forms as outlined on p. 34. Various foods such as *milk* and various meal-times such as *tea* (though such words may at first be identified as the food a baby has at that meal rather than the actual meal-time itself) are also important.

A baby will also learn the parts of its body, particularly *face*, *fingers* and *toes*, and the first two will be familiar to it from its immediate family. Clothes and toys will be immediately relevant to a child and so words like *sock* and *teddy* are likely to be learned early. Then a child will learn words for parts of the house and household items, words for animals, particularly domestic ones, and words which enable it to function socially like *yes* and *no* and *please* and *thank you*. Soon words attached to actions will be learned, though whether a child thinks of them as action words or simply formulas which accompany a particular action, such as *bye-bye* which is used when daddy or mummy leaves in the morning, is debatable. After that it will go on to learn some words indicating place such as *there* and *on* and words that describe some of the other words it has learned such as *hot* or *red*.

By the time it is eighteen months old the average child may have learned approximately fifty words. A few studies have recorded the first fifty words of individual children, and the following list is that recorded for an American girl:

baby;	mommy;	doggie;	juice;	bye-bye;
daddy;	milk;	cracker;	done;	ball;
shoe;	teddy;	book;	kitty;	hi;
Alex;	no;	door;	dolly;	what's that;
cheese;	oh wow;	oh;	button;	eye;
apple;	nose;	bird;	alldone;	orange;
bottle;	coat;	hot;	bib;	hat;
more;	ear;	night-night;	paper;	toast;
O'Toole;	bath;	down;	duck;	leaf;
cookie;	lake;	car;	rock;	box.

The compilation of similar lists of the first fifty or hundred words could be productive.

Speed of learning vocabulary

Although children acquire their vocabulary at different ages, there is a pattern which emerges from those studies which have been done. Little or no vocabulary is learned in the first year. At the end of the first year and the beginning of the second a child learns a few words rather slowly. From a base of about ten words it will possibly acquire a further twenty in the first months of its second year (from 1;0 to 1;5).

During the second half of its second year it is likely to add to its vocabulary much more quickly, so that by the time it is two it may well have a vocabulary of eighty words. It must be emphasised though that it is difficult to be certain how many words a child knows. Like most of us a child's passive vocabulary may be larger than its active one, and it is not always easy to find out what its passive vocabulary may consist of. In most studies of a child's vocabulary a word is taken in its very simplest sense of a series of sounds which are repeated in the same pattern and usually has no reference to meaning. If a child uses the same 'word' to mean several different things or in several different contexts, the form is understood to be only one word. Equally word counts bear no relation to how much a child speaks, and studies distinguishing between **word types** (the number of individual words) and **word tokens** (the number of times an individual word is used) are needed.

After the end of the second year the acquisition of vocabulary becomes much more rapid and is linked to the ability to join words together into **meaningful sequences**. A growing interest in the world around it and an ability to make sense at a more abstract level and to ask questions naturally promote a sharp rise in the number of words a child knows.

The growth in a child's vocabulary is also linked to its increasing awareness that words have a 'correct' meaning, because this awareness generates the need to acquire more vocabulary. A realisation that the word *car* means only a mechanised vehicle to carry up to five persons generates the need to acquire words like *red*, if the child had associated redness with the word *car* because the family car is red, and *bus* and *lorry*, which may be mechanised vehicles but represent types of vehicle which are quite different from *car*. The tendency to overextend the meaning of words is very characteristic of children in their second year, but as they reach the age of three they usually understand that words are more restricted in meaning than they had supposed and learn additional vocabulary to compensate.

It is difficult if not impossible to calculate with any accuracy the growth in vocabulary after the age of two, simply because the rate of growth is so rapid and the number of words involved is so large that counting is difficult. By the age of three many children have a vocabulary of at least 1,000 words, for in their third year they are subject to many more verbal stimuli and they can participate much more fully in dialogues. Many children during this year learn that words can have more than one meaning, that a *tape*, for instance, can be something which plays music as well as something sown on to clothes. Children at this stage ask a lot of questions as part of their process of getting to grips with the world around them; and many of these questions take the form 'What is that called?'.

We should also remember that children are not passive learners of vocabulary. They are prepared to invent words of their own, partly because they cannot pronounce the sounds which they hear, and partly because they extend the meaning of words. Many children have an inventive attitude to the words they hear and use. Children play with words in their learning process.

Because children learn mostly nouns at first, in their third year they will have catching up to do in the acquisition of verbs, adjectives and grammatical words. At first words like *up* may be used as verbs or as whole utterances in the sense 'put it up there'. Then a child may learn verbs like *put* and *take*. It is interesting that they often use such verbs correctly at first because they are used in very restricted contexts. As they try to extend the range of contexts in which verbs are used, they may be confused so that *put* and *take* are used with the same apparent meaning. Naturally the acquisition of grammatical words is dependent upon the growth of a child's learning of syntax. The ability to organise a sentence properly is also tied up with morphology and the deployment of such features as different tenses of the verbs.

SYNTAX

The acquisition of syntax by children is a difficult subject to handle because it is not clear whether adult categories are the ones which should be applied to the language of children. Syntax involves learning the various forms of a word, such as *sing/sang* or *boy/boys*, and how they should be deployed in a sentence. It also means recognising the function of grammatical words, and organising lexical and grammatical words in a meaningful order not only within a phrase but also within clauses. It also means having a sufficient vocabulary to provide the meaning for the grammatical pattern which is constructed. Naturally this takes time.

The morphology of English, the different forms that a word can take because of its function or meaning, is not as complicated as that of some languages, but the morphology of the spoken language a child hears may differ according to the speakers it is exposed to, though this is not likely to be a major factor before the age of three. The process of **analogy**, whereby irregular forms are assimilated to the dominant pattern, is a feature of many children's language as it is of some adults'. All plurals will end in -*s* to give *foots* and *mans*, all verbs will have a past tense in -*ed* to give *putted* and *comed*, and all adjectives will form their comparative by using *more* to give *more red* and *more high*. But coming to terms with such anomalies is not a great problem since they have tended to survive in English only in very common words, because the less common ones succumbed to the influence of analogy long ago.

It is possible to claim that most utterances that children make are functionally effective though they are not grammatically perfect. This is partly because their needs are relatively few and mostly context bound, like eating, sleeping or having a nappy change, and partly because their parents are willing to spend a lot of time in decoding the message which the grammatically incomplete utterance conveys. Single words can readily be interpreted as embodying a more complex utterance: *give* may mean 'give me the toy' and *gone* may mean 'I have eaten all my food and so I am a good boy'. Whether they do have the meanings we attribute to them is not easy to decide, for children go on to learn more complex utterances as though such simple one-word sentences are not enough for their communicative needs.

From a single word utterance to a complex sentence a child will go through several stages. The following are some that can be traced in this progression: two-word utterances; simple phrases; simple clauses; and compound/complex sentences.

Two-word utterances

It is often said that the use of two-word utterances is the beginning of a child's learning of syntax. Such utterances begin at about eighteen months and go through three steps, often fairly quickly. At first the utterances can be random and have no fixed order so that *all gone* and *gone all* interchange in no very discernible pattern. Then a regular pattern emerges, *all gone*, which is repeated frequently but which is not productive in the sense that it does not generate similar two-word utterances. The final stage is reached when other utterances are based on this pattern to give examples like *all lost* or *mummy gone*. There are several constructions within these two-word utterances.

• The first is determiner plus noun as in *my teddy*, *her teddy* and *that teddy*. It is possible that other utterances like *teddy drink* or *mummy hat* are based on this pattern with the use of a possessive noun instead of the determiner (though in the first example *drink* may be a verb rather than a noun).

• The second is a noun, often an agent, plus verb as in *milk gone*, *sock gone* and *baby cry*. Some examples which might be thought to contain a possessive plus another noun such as *baby bed* may actually imply a noun plus verb in the sense 'baby is going to bed'.

• A third is a verb followed by another part of speech which may be a direct or indirect object or an adverb of place as in *drink milk*, *give me*, and *look there*.

• A fourth is where an object, a noun or pronoun, is defined in some way such as *red car*, *funny dog*, *she silly*.

These patterns as already implied may be interpreted in several ways because the child has no mechanism for expressing the grammatical relationship of the two words which form an utterance. A two-word utterance like *dog look* could be interpreted to mean 'The dog is looking at us', 'Please look at the dog', or even 'Please, dog, look at that'. Similarly a phrase like *Granny car* could mean 'Granny's car', 'Granny is coming by car', 'Granny is going by car', or 'Granny is driving the car'. In some cases the context will help to explicate the meaning, though anyone who has talked with young children knows that it can be difficult to understand precisely what they are trying to say. Since we do not know what a child's thought processes are, we cannot tell what it considers important to relate in speech. We are prone to assume that it is saying what we think it should be saying.

Two-word utterances are extremely important because they represent the first stage in recognising that words can **interrelate** and that the meaning of one word may be altered by adding other words to it. At first it may well be true that children accept a two-word utterance as simply a longer word, so that *black dog* is simply a category of object. Only when they can separate *black* and *dog* and use each word in separate combinations will they discover that each represents a distinct concept which can be combined with other concepts. At the same time two-word utterances encourage the understanding of **morphological structure**. The use of the morpheme *-s* to indicate a plural develops at this time so that the distinction between one and more than one becomes meaningful. The difference between some parts of the verb begins to be acquired so that *Daddy go* and *Daddy gone* are seen to embody different time referents. The use of adverbials made of prepositions occurs in two-word utterances such as *in bed* or *on bed*, and from these children begin to learn the function of grammatical words.

Other developments

From the two-word utterance a child goes on to construct more complicated sequences and also learns how to handle such things as the verb phrase, negation and questions.

• From two words a child progresses naturally to **three-word** utterances which often involve an agent, an action and the recipient such as *Daddy make tea*, though in this sentence *Daddy* may be understood to be a form of address rather than the subject of *make*. It is then possible to develop the two-noun phrases by adding premodifiers or postmodifiers and to develop the verb phrase by auxiliaries. Indeed some auxiliaries appear in the negative long before they are used in the positive forms: *can't go* is more common among young children than *can go*. The use of *do* with negation also encourages the early acquisition of that auxiliary.

• The earliest **negative form** is likely to be *no*, though it is possible that before then a /n/ sound may indicate negation. *No* is used because it occurs frequently as an answer to a yes–no question or to a command. A request like *It's time to go to bed now* may well be met with the response *no*. A simple negation of this type is usually acquired earlier than negatives which deal with some feature of non-existence such as *There are no apples today*. Because *no* is acquired early it is extended to other negative uses and it occurs as the sentence negative marker instead of *not* or *not* with the auxiliary. *No come* is more likely to be used as an early negative than either *not come* or *don't come*. In two-word utterances it is natural that *no* should be used as one of the two words: *no come* or *no bed*. As sentences grow longer than two words then negation develops with it so that negatives are used more in accord with adult practice.

• Asking **questions** may start at about the same time as negation is introduced into a child's language. Children are naturally curious and they want to find out what the world around them consists of. Questions, like negation, can be expressed through a single word, particularly those beginning with *wh-*. But when the two-word stage is reached it is possible for children to ask recognisable questions within this structure: *Where Daddy? Where dollie? When home? Why bed?* From there it is a relatively easy step to introduce an **agent** in a three-word sentence: *why me bed? where Mummy gone?* Questions which expect a *yes* or *no* answer may start even earlier and be indicated through tone of voice, though it may be difficult to decide whether a question is intended or not. Something like *this mine* may be a question asking whether it is mine or it may be a statement claiming it is mine. Even with questions introduced by a *wh-* word, inversion which would make the nature of the question clear may not appear till much later than the use of the actual *wh-* word.

• Once a child has learned to construct sentences of an **SVO** structure and has learned to elaborate each part of that structure, it can then proceed to build more complex sentences by introducing a **second clause**. This involves learning the meaning of various conjunctions and how to organise the clauses within a complex sentence. Of course certain relations between clauses can be expressed by *and* as well as by subordinating conjunctions, and that applies particularly to time relationships. *It stopped raining and we went out* can express the same meaning as *When it stopped raining we went out*. Narrative sequence is expressed by *and*, which can also imply a temporal or even a causal relation. At this level it is difficult to introduce any general stages which reflect all children's progress, because there is considerable diversity in how each child acquires the competence to use this kind of grammatical structure. Far fewer studies have been undertaken of the learning process at this stage than at earlier stages, partly because there is so much more data which would need to be collected.

ANALYSIS OF CHILD TALK

It is time now to consider some passages of child talk to see the features that have been outlined above in a more extended sequence of discourse. The first passage is from a monologue recorded of a girl, Emily, during her second year. This and other monologues were recorded as she was alone at night in her cot before she fell asleep. The monologue is recorded in Katherine Nelson (ed.), *Narratives from the Crib* (Cambridge, MA: Havard University Press, 1989), p. 158. In this monologue Emily was 1;9(8) and is talking to her doll.

```
        baby no in night
        cause baby crying
        baby in might
        baby in might
        my baby no in my car                            5
        my baby in my
        baby no eat supper in in in this
        no eat broccoli no
        so my baby have dinner
        then baby get sick                              10
        baby no eat dinner
        broccoli soup carrots cause rice
        baby eat that
        baby no in night
        broccoli broccoli soup cabbage carrots          15
        no baby sleeping
        so why baby eat
        then baby get sick
        Emmy no eat dinner
        broccoli soup cause                             20
        no baby sleeping
        baby sleeping all night
```

• The passage is given in standardised spelling and so it is not possible to comment on the sounds which Emily made, other than she appears to use *might* for *night* (ll. 4–5), though *night* is recorded at ll. 1 and 14.

• As far as vocabulary is concerned the passage is, as one might expect, very repetitive so that there is a high proportion of words which are repeated. The ratio of word tokens to word types is much greater than one would expect in an adult conversation. There are sixteen examples of *baby*, five of *broccoli* and of *night* (taking *might* as representing *night*), five of *eat* and three of *sleeping*, and eight of *no*.

The vocabulary contains words which are surprising in the vocabulary of a child of twenty-one months, but words like *broccoli*, *cabbage* and *rice* may occur because they were regular in the family's meals or because they were all mentioned at the meal which preceded the monologue and had been used so frequently at the meal that they stuck in her mind.

• Apart from these words for particular types of food which reflect the eating habits of the family, the words are largely of the type one might expect. *Baby*, which means the doll, occurs frequently because it is the actor of the narrative and is thus the agent subject of most of the utterances. *Supper* and *dinner*, which appear to be interchangeable, occur because of the subject matter of the monologue, which naturally includes the verb *eat* and the names of the foods to be eaten. The word *sick* one might expect to occur in an American baby's vocabulary since it represents a topic of concern to all parents. The word *night* and the action word *sleeping* are also common in children's language and occur here because the child is in her cot.

• Most of the words are nouns, though there are a few verbs and an occasional adjective. Some grammatical words are to be found, but their role is not always very clear. *In* appears to be used in accordance with adult usage, but the meaning of *cause* is less certain. The negator *no* occurs often, for it is a word which parents use frequently to their children and which they in turn use as frequently in their playing the role of a mummy to their doll. There are few determiners, but *my* occurs three times and *this* and *that* once each. The referents of *this* and *that* are not explicit. Only one word seems totally out of place in the monologue and that is *car*, since the role-playing appears to repeat a scene at the dinner table. Its occurrence may reflect the importance of a car in this family and the frequency of its use in family conversations.

• In morphology we may note that the verb occurs in two forms: one the base form of the verb *eat* and *get,* and the other the present participle *crying* and *sleeping.* There is no *-s* ending to indicate the third person of the present indicative and there is no auxiliary with the present participle. Since the verbs in *-ing* are different from those in the base form it is not possible to tell from this passage whether Emily understood that *-ing* was a morphological ending which could be attached to other verbs. Whether a form like *crying* is a verb meaning 'cries, is crying' is also uncertain, but probable. The *-s* plural form exists in *carrots,* but whether Emily recognised this as a plural is less certain. To her it may have appeared that *carrots* was a single concept like *broccoli* and *soup* which existed only in that form.

• Syntactically one may notice embryonic sentences with an SVO structure such as *baby no eat supper* and *baby get sick.* But many sentences do not have this degree of structure because one of the three elements is missing. The verb is missing in *my baby no in my car,* and as we have seen there are no auxiliaries. The subject is missing in *no eat broccoli no;* and the object is missing in *so why baby eat,* and possibly in *baby eat that.* Sometimes two elements are missing and so it is impossible to decide whether there is a string of nouns in an arbitrary fashion or whether they together formed some meaning in Emily's mind, as in *broccoli broccoli soup cabbage carrots.*

There are few determiners and most nouns appear without them. *My* occurs twice before *baby,* but *baby* is usually introduced without *my* or any other determiner. There are no examples of *your* or *her.* The preposition *in* occurs in its correct place before a noun or pronoun, but it is sometimes repeated as *in in in this.* The negator *no* often occurs in front of a verb, but if the verb is missing it may appear where one might expect the verb (*baby no in night*) or rather more randomly within the sentence (*no baby sleeping*). The word *cause* (for *because*) is known and used, but its function is clearly not yet assimilated for it appears quite arbitrarily in utterances. Emily has not got to the stage where she can form complex sentences, but one can see that a first step in that general direction has been taken.

The second passage records a dialogue between a young boy, Mark, and his mother when they are both in the kitchen. Mark is waiting for his mother to finish the dishes so that she can play with him. The passage is taken from Gordon Wells, *The Meaning Makers* (London: Hodder & Stoughton, 1987), pp. 26–7.

Mark: Play. Play. Play, Mummy. Mummy, come on.
Mother: All right.
Mark: Helen play, please? [*He wants his sister to play with him, too*] Helen still in bed, Mummy?
Mother: [*From the next room.*] Mm?
Mark: Helen still – Helen still gone sleep, Mummy?
Mother: No. She's up there talking, isn't she?
Mark: Yes. Helen come down? [request]
[*Mother finally comes to play with him. A few minutes later, Mark is playing with a collection of toy cars, running them down a ramp from the roof of his garage*]
[*Referring to one of his toys*] Top of the coach [bus]. Broken.
Mother: Who broke the coach?
Mark: Mark did.
Mother: How?
Mark: Out.
Mother: How did you break it?
Mark: Dunno [I don't know]. [4-second pause] Mend it, Mummy.
Mother: I can't, darling.
Mark: All right.
Mother: Look the wheels have gone as well.
Mark: Oh! I want Daddy take it to work ∩ mend it.
Mother: [*checking*] Daddy did?
Mark: Daddy take it away – take it to work ∩ mend it.*
Mother: You'll have to ask him, won't you.
Mark: Yeh, You do it [ask him].

*The sign ∩ indicates a short gap.

• Once again this exchange is written in standardised spelling and so it is not possible to tell whether Mark had any difficulty in pronouncing the words he used, though at his age and with his background one might assume that that was unlikely. The word *Mummy* is presumably pronounced in an adult way.

• The **vocabulary** is relatively simple, for the exchange revolves around playing, his toys and his sister Helen. Most of the words Mark uses are monosyllabic and the nouns are concrete. There are a number of verbs and some adverbs but there are no adjectives. The verbs show an important growth in vocabulary and Mark can distinguish between the phrasal verbs *come on* and *come down*. There is still quite a large element of repetition with four examples of *play* and three of *still*. But these repetitions are more for emphasis and to get his message across than for lack of vocabulary. Mark is now familiar with pronouns and is clearly developing an understanding of how to relate utterances to people; he uses *I, you, she* and *it*.

• The **verb forms** are more advanced than in the first passage. Mark uses the base form of the verb most frequently, but he is beginning to tackle more complicated verb forms though he has yet to sort them out properly. He can say *Helen still gone sleep* with *gone* in the past participle and *sleep* in the base form; together they seem to represent a complex verb form with *gone* as a kind of auxiliary meaning 'Is she still asleep?' or 'Has she gone to sleep?'. But he can use the verb *want* with a following non-finite complement clause even though it has not been arranged absolutely in accord with adult grammar.

• **Syntactically** he uses short sentences, which are largely simple in construction though he appears to understand that a more complex sentence structure is possible. He uses *play* as a command, but whether he understands the difference between the structure of a statement and of a command is uncertain. He uses sentences like *Play; Play. Mummy*; and *Helen play?*, the first of which is a command and the second is presumably meant to be so, though it may be meant more as a statement as either 'Mummy play' or 'I play, Mummy'. The third is interpreted by Wells as a question presumably because of the intonation which Mark used, but it has the form of a statement. It does not have the inversion associated with questions and it has no auxiliary; and for this reason one may wonder whether the other sentences are more statements than commands.

Equally the sentence *Mummy, come on* is punctuated as though it is a question, though it may have been meant by Mark as a declarative *Mummy come on*. When Mark says *I want daddy take it to work ⌒ mend it*, he probably understands *mend it* to be 'Daddy mend it'. Whether he understands *Mend it, Mummy* in the same way or as a command is less easy to decide. His final *You do it* is a command though it has a statement form. What is clear is that he can have sentences with the subject in the first position and sentences either without a subject or with the subject in a final position as though a form of address. He is clearly experimenting with word order and is coming to an understanding of different sentence structures even if he has not achieved a complete grasp of the various structures as yet.

• Mark is clearly familiar with sentences which have an **agent as subject** because that also allows him to have a simple verb, either in the base form or in the past tense as in *did*. Most sentences have an agent subject, either a noun or pronoun, or they have no subject at all. He is not familiar with the passive and so he expresses 'The top of the coach is broken' as two separate utterances *Top of the coach. Broken.* He sees the semantic link between the two, but cannot yet express it in an adult grammatical way. What is important to note is that he knows how to construct a noun phrase to give the structure *Top of the coach* consisting of the head and a postmodifier which is itself a prepositional phrase. Equally he can construct a fairly complex non-finite complement clause in *take it to work*. The grammatical relationship of *mend it* to the previous clause is uncertain though the general meaning relationship is clear. Was Mark trying to say *to mend it*; or *I want him to mend it*; or *he will mend it*? Several possibilities exist because the grammatical relationship is not expressed in any way. Indeed, Mark's syntax is often based on the principle of putting two statements together and leaving the relation between them to be inferred by the listener.

These are some of the points which you can look for in passages of child language, but there are many different aspects of language acquisition which naturally have not been covered in these examples.

EXERCISES

The following two passages are also taken from Gordon Wells, *The Meaning Makers*, and may be used for analysis of the language. The first passage (pp. 23–4) is an earlier stage in the dialogue between Mark and his mother.

[*Mark is in the living room with his mother. He is standing by a radiator*]

Mark:	'Ot, Mummy?	
Mother:	Hot? Yes, that's the radiator.	
Mark:	Been – burn?	
Mother:	Burn?	5
Mark:	Yeh.	
Mother:	Yes, you know it'll burn, don't you?	
Mark:	[*putting hand on radiator*] Oh! Ooh!	
Mother:	Take your hand off of it.	
Mark:	Uh?	10
Mother:	[*asking if he needs his other shoelace tied*] What about the other shoe?	
Mark:	It all done, Mummy.	
Mother:	Mm?	
Mark:	It done, Mummy.	15
Mother:	It's done, is it?	
Mark:	Yeh.	
Mother:	Oh. [*Mark tries to get up to see out of the window.*]	
Mother:	No! Leave the curtains.	
Mark:	Oh, up please.	20
Mother:	Leave the curtain, please.	
Mark:	No.	
Mother:	Leave the curtain, Mark.	
Mark:	No. [*Looking out of window, he sees a man digging in his garden*] A man – a man er – dig down there.	25
Mother:	A man walked down there?	
Mark:	Yeh.	

* * *

The second passage (p. 62) is a dialogue between Rosie, age 5, and her mother, while watching a television programme about making pots.

Rosie:	[*referring to the potter's wheel*] Mum, what – what's making it go round?
Mother:	Er – well, like a clock.
Rosie:	Er?
Mother:	A clock.

Rosie:	What clock?	5
	[*Mother does not reply. 30 second pause.*]	
Mother:	They're digging	
Rosie:	Why they dig – ? Why? Why *they* dig – ?	
Mother:	*That's* for the boilers.	
Rosie:	Er? Why's the boy *digging*? Why's the boy – ?	10
Mother:	*Well*, they're shoveling it into a machine.	
Rosie:	Er? Why they tipping it into the 'chine – machine?	
Mother:	They'll tell you now.	
	[*Commentator explains what is happening*]	
	Oh! that's clay.	15
	[*Picture shows molds being made*]	
Rosie:	Er? Clay?	
Mother:	There it is. Look, they're saucepans – not sauce-pans. What do you call them? Basins. It looks like basins, doesn't it? I think that's a cup. For plates and that, look.	20
Rosie:	Er? Is there toilet rolls?	
Mother:	No. That's a cup.	
Rosie:	Why they trying to do that for?	

* * *

ESSAY QUESTIONS

We now include some questions which could be used for class discussion or for essay work.

1 Examine either of the passages on pp. 52–3 and analyse the vocabulary in terms of the types and tokens used by the child.
2 Examine the fifty words given on p. 39 and quantify how many words fall into each word class (noun, verb, etc.). Discuss how far the numbers you arrive at match what you might expect the distribution to be.
3 Consider the following two-word utterances and discuss what their structure is and what their meaning may be:

baby lie;
dolly toy;
daddy drink;

it gone;
she finger;
where there.

4 Explain why you think a child may pronounce the following
   words in the way each is represented:

   banana   /*nana*/
   chip   /*tɪ*/
   truck   /*tʌk*/
   take   /*kek*/
   water   /*wawa*/.

5 Discuss the stages a child might go through as it learns how to
   ask a question.
6 Discuss the stages a child might go through as it learns how to
   express negation.
7 Explain what you consider to be the average language
   attainment of a child at twenty-four months.
8 What parallels can you find between child language acquisition and the historical development of English?
9 Comment on the influence of analogy in child language
   acquisition.

3
Language Change

INTRODUCTION

All living languages change, which is why every generation produces its crop of complaints about what is usually thought of as the 'corruption' of the language, for as we get older we resent the way the language is being changed by younger people. It is particularly vocabulary which attracts the wrath of those who believe that language should be kept 'pure', though language changes in every feature: spelling, punctuation, sounds, morphology, syntax, word-formation and vocabulary.

From this list it will be appreciated that both the written and the spoken forms of English change and have changed over the years. From a historical point of view it is particularly the written variety which is our concern since before the invention of tape recorders there was no easy way of recording speech and historical texts are available to us only in a written form, even if some of them claim to represent the spoken language by using what its authors claim is a more phonetic alphabet.

• In commenting on historical change one is likely to assume a contrast between the language as it exists today and as it existed at the time of the text under examination. The features that strike one in the latter are those that differ from Modern English. But remember that 'English' is a concept which embraces many different forms including **regional** and **class varieties**. In the Introduction we noted the two sentences '*E were right gormless* and *He was absolutely stupid*. Different varieties of English like these have existed throughout its history, and one must take care if one is comparing a past text with a modern one to make sure that both are written in a similar style and variety of language.

Within written texts there are many different genres: poetry, novels, documents and letters, to name only a few. Letters are likely to have an informal style which is quite different from documents, which often have a stilted syntax and specialised vocabulary. Poetry was until recently more formal than prose and had an appropriate style. The novel may contain informal elements in its representation of speech, but it may also contain elaborate and formal descriptions. It is important to be aware of the genre of the text you are studying because this will dictate some of the linguistic characteristics it has. In any study of the language of an older text, a comparison should ideally be with the language of an equivalent genre today. If that is not possible allowances should always be made for the differences in genre. The genre of the text as well as its date will dictate what features of language are significant and need comment.

• In addition to different genres English has many regional varieties or dialects. For the most part these can be ignored for your purposes since they form a rather specialised aspect of the history of English. Before the standardisation of the language began in the fifteenth century and particularly with the onset of printing, texts were written and copied in many localised forms although some of these showed some degree of standardisation. It is unlikely that you would need to consider any text written before printing was introduced into England in 1476.

With the introduction of printing the process of standardisation developed and this means historically that there is a tendency to eliminate variety in the standard written language. This affects spelling most, but even in matters like morphology, syntax and vocabulary it is a potent force. Generally when people say something is not 'correct English', it means they disapprove of a variant which they think is not part of the standard written language. Since speech can never be standardised as much as writing, it is usually the introduction of variants from the spoken level into writing which arouses this type of reaction.

• Language is a reflection of the society it serves, of its concerns and interests. This applies as much to English as to any other language, and the written varieties of English will all be affected by prevailing attitudes even if to differing degrees. Often such attitudes will be a reaction against those which were predominant in the preceding age: an insistence on correctness may be followed by a more tolerant attitude to variety.

* In the Tudor and Elizabethan periods the rise of **nationalism** affected the language. An optimistic thrusting nation needs an appropriate language. But English had been considered by many a less elegant and expressive language than Latin or even French. It was therefore desirable to enlarge its vocabulary and thus the general esteem in which it was held. A large number of new words entered the language, either borrowed from Latin or continental countries or introduced from the new lands being discovered. This attitude affected **style** which became rather pompous in the rush to introduce polysyllabic words and rhetorical effects.

* A reaction set in during the seventeenth century influenced by the growth of Puritanism and the development of the new science. A distrust of rhetoric led to the call for a more factual language which would be simpler, more logical and less verbose. During the eighteenth century the growth of rationality in the so-called Age of Reason with its emphasis on order and priority had its own impact on the language. Many wanted to purify the language and then to fix it. This desire prompted the development of a **standardised grammar**, with its notions of correctness and thus put emphasis on the learning of rules. Grammar became an educational attainment and the status of non-standard varieties declined ever more sharply. The rules which have tormented young children until recently, such as not using *It's me*, were largely invented at this time, often on the basis of what was permissible in Latin. Indeed, 'grammar' as a term came increasingly to mean not so much how a language operated as how a language **ought to operate**; in other words 'grammar' and 'good grammar' came to be virtually synonymous. Since that time the nature of English has been closely linked with the rules of grammar and politicians in particular often call for a return to the proper standards of English, by which they mean the observance of what they understand to be the rules of grammar.

* The Romantic Revolution, whose beginning in England is associated with the publication of the *Lyrical Ballads* in 1798, directed people's attention once more to the regional and class varieties of English, an interest which was strengthened throughout the nineteenth century. People were anxious to record the language of the peasants of Cumbria or of the working class in London before it disappeared entirely in the face of the growth of education and the spread of learning lower down the social scale.

But the new concern for different varieties did not disturb the preeminent position of Standard English as the true end of all education, even if the different varieties were increasingly represented in novels, plays and even poetry.

★ The Victorian admiration for the past and the establishment of the British Empire meant many archaic as well as new words entered the language. The need to educate the people of the empire meant that Standard English and received pronunciation (the prestige pronunciation – in fact a variety of Southern English – which is regarded by many as correct and the sign of an educated person) were taught widely and received widespread recognition.

★ The twentieth century has witnessed a loosening of the stranglehold of the standard language. The loss of empire, the concern to do justice to ethnic minorities and to re-establish the confidence of former colonial nations, the growth of linguistics which recognised that different varieties of English are not corrupt versions of the standard but independent varieties often with a long history, and the desire to let young people develop confidence in their communicative ability by expressing themselves in their own variety have all prompted the raising of the status of the non-standard varieties of English. The general lifting of many of the inhibitions in social attitudes has allowed the boundaries between formal and informal English to change dramatically so that the so-called four-letter words like *shit* are frequently seen in print today even in what is recognised as serious literature.

When examining the language of a historical text, you should remember these general attitudes, because they may affect how an author writes and what he is trying to achieve through his style.

ELEMENTS OF LANGUAGE

It is time now to look at the various elements of language to illustrate the kind of feature you should look out for in examining a text. The following list should not be treated as comprehensive, an impossible task in a short chapter, or even as a model for the way in which to approach a historical text. It provides examples of the things to notice, but texts from different periods will have certain points that need particular consideration and others which can be ignored.

Spelling

In the early days of printing different spellings were tolerated and that tolerance continued for a long time in less formal writing.

• To some extent therefore the history of spelling is the history of the reduction of variants, but not all variants have been eliminated from the language. For example, it is still possible to write words like *galvanise* with *-ise* or with *-ize*; American English always uses the latter. Variants were far commoner in the past. Thus internally in a word *i* could vary with *y*, as in *write/wryte* or *quite/quyte*, whereas at the end of the word the variation was more likely to be between *-ie* and *-y*, as in *magnifie/magnify*. Similarly a syllable with a short vowel could end with a single consonant, a double consonant or a double consonant plus *e*, as in *ship/shipp/shippe* or *worship/worshipp/worshippe*. Long vowels could be written in a variety of forms: the vowel could be doubled, have an *e* added, or have an *e* added after a single consonant. Thus modern *feet* and *wife* could vary with older *fete* and *wiif*; and the two methods could be combined in *goose*, which varied with *gose* and *goos* formerly. The use of *e* after a vowel to indicate length is less common, but survives in a word like *gruesome*, but was in the past more frequent. The same variety applies to long vowels at the end of words: *do* could be spelt *do*, *doo* or *doe*.

• The elimination of variants has not always been straightforward so that as variants were shed we were left only with the modern spelling, for sometimes it seemed as though a different spelling might become standard. For much of the seventeenth and eighteenth centuries it looked as though the standard spelling of words like *music* would be in *-ick* rather than in *-ic*; and in the seventeenth century final *-l* in words like *magical* appeared more often as *-ll* than as *-l*. Bear in mind that such spellings in older texts may represent the regular form then whereas the modern forms may well have been irregular. In modern times spelling has become something of a shibboleth, but attitudes were much more relaxed before the middle of the eighteenth century. Even today writers of informal letters may be less conscious of spelling and may also be prepared to use a large number of abbreviations such as *cd.* for *could,* & for *and* or *wh* for *which.*

Punctuation

Although modern spelling admits few variants, modern punctuation is much less regulated and it is more difficult to determine what is 'correct'. The history of punctuation is partly the record of the introduction of new punctuation marks and partly the change in their use and frequency. A few marks have dropped out of use. Do remember that many older texts appear in modern editions in modern punctuation and use marks which may not have been available when the text was first written.

• A mark that has disappeared is the slash (/) which in early printed books often took the role of a comma. In the early sixteenth century punctuation was relatively light, but at the end of the century and in the seventeenth century punctuation could be used rather heavily – a tendency which coincided with the introduction of new marks. The colon (:) was frequently used at this time and had a greater range of significance than today. Its role was partly replaced by the semi-colon (;). Other marks which may have been known earlier but which became frequent at this time include brackets, the dash, the question mark and the exclamation mark.

• An important difference between earlier and modern punctuation is that the former is used for **rhetorical** purposes, particularly to help the reader to know where to pause if reading aloud, whereas the latter is more **grammatical** in its application, i.e. to mark off grammatical units such as clauses and sentences. Because of its rhetorical nature modern readers often find older punctuation puzzling and apparently arbitrary. Even capital letters may be used to note emphasis, which is why they may be found on many nouns in older texts.

Sounds

The standardisation of spelling means that it is not possible to trace sounds in most texts, though some letters and examples of non-standard speech may suggest certain differences in sound from received pronunciation.

Morphology

Under this heading pay particular attention to differences in **inflectional endings**. In the present tense of the verb there is an older form in *-est, thou comest,* and the variation between *-eth/-(e)s, he cometh/comes.* The *-est* forms drop out as the plural *you* takes over the singular role as well, and the *-eth* form gives way to *-(e)s* except in certain genres, such as biblical language. The difference between *-eth* and *-(e)s* may be stylistic or, in poetry, metrical. Other verb forms may also show variation; the past participle may be either *-en* or *-ed* in some verbs. Nouns too show variation. The plural form in *-(e)s* extends to those nouns which had had plural in *-en* or no inflectional ending at all.

Syntax

This is the most difficult section to cover adequately since it embraces so many different aspects.

• One important feature is **word order**, which is freer in earlier periods than today with variation in the order of the various parts of a clause as well as within individual phrases such as the noun phrase. There is also a tendency in English to increase the number of grammatical words in sentences so that the relationship between clauses and phrases is explicit rather than implicit.

• The number of **conjunctions** and **prepositions** has grown. For example, a causal relationship where one clause expresses the reason for what happens as expressed in another clause may be implicit where today it would be explicit through the use of a conjunction like *because* or *for.* In *The Merchant of Venice* the sentence *This Hebrew will turne Christian, he growes kind* (I.3.173) probably has a causal sense 'This Hebrew will turn into a Christian because he is growing generous'. The second clause expresses the reason for what is stated in the first one.

• Many **verbs** are worth noting. The use of *do* and modal auxiliaries has grown since the fifteenth century. In Shakespeare's time *do* was a stylistic marker of formal or pompous style, whereas today it is grammaticalised in interrogative and negative sentences and is used elsewhere for emphasis. The modal auxiliaries like *can* and *must* are more frequent today, particularly in various combinations. This means that the simple verb often carried the meaning in the past that an auxiliary does now.

• Negation can be expressed in different ways in earlier English. A double or triple negative is not uncommon, and before the eighteenth century it was not necessarily regarded as incorrect. The negative word could also appear in different positions and was still used at first with the simple verb, e.g. *he comes not, he not comes*. In many similar cases the grammarians of the eighteenth century chose one variant to be standard and reduced the other variants to the status of being incorrect. Thus in the sixteenth century *lovelier* and *more lovelier* were both acceptable; but the eighteenth century made the latter incorrect. So in syntax as in spelling you will find more variation the further back you go, but do not assume that these variants were regarded in the way we see them today.

• Other features which show interesting developments include the **relative pronoun**. The use of *who, which* and *that* changes throughout English, as does the use of the zero form (i.e. no relative pronoun at all). But there are many other features which it is not possible to mention here.

Word-formation

Two features will be highlighted in this section: compounds and the use of affixes (i.e. prefixes and suffixes).

• **Compounds,** when two words are joined together to form a new word as in *skyscraper*, have been common at all periods, though attitudes towards them have changed. Sometimes they have been considered very poetic, and at others rather more colloquial particularly in relation to some technical items. Compounds are more likely to be nouns and adjectives, though other parts of speech are not excluded.

• The range of **prefixes** and **suffixes** has been reduced over the history of English, particularly in verbs. Prefixes like *be-, de-* and *to-* are much less frequent than they were, partly because verbs have developed as phrasal verbs such as *run down, wind up*. Some prefixes and suffixes have become more popular like *non-* as in *non-combatant* and *-free* as in *genderfree*. At an earlier period suffixes were more interchangeable than now so that *wisdom* could vary with *wiseness*; today a single form survives.

Vocabulary

The English vocabulary has undergone profound changes over the last five hundred years. Some words have dropped out of the language, others have been introduced, and many have changed their meaning. You will come across words no longer extant or whose meaning has changed.

• Often **change in meaning** precedes loss from the language. The word *swink* has been replaced by *labour* and *toil*. With the introduction of these new words *swink* became specialised in meaning to 'sexual work, i.e. sexual intercourse' and thus became informal and ultimately disappeared. Many words were introduced from Latin and this has affected the original English words, usually through specialisation or loss. *Worthy* and its derivatives are now less often used, and their place is taken by words like *excellent* and *noble*. The presence of *pure* has restricted *clean* to physical as distinct from spiritual or abstract matters. *Strife* has been largely displaced by *contest* and other words.

• The commonest way of increasing the vocabulary is by **borrowing** words from other languages. Often this is a matter of style and fashion so that words are borrowed from approved languages like Latin or French; but words may be borrowed for technical reasons because there is a new object or concept to be referred to and such words may be borrowed from the languages from which the object was borrowed like *tomato* and *bungalow*. You should try to recognise not only the language from which a word is borrowed but also why it is borrowed from that language. New words can be invented through **compounding** (see pp. 3–5) and through **functional shift**, by which a word in one part of speech is used as another part of speech, e.g. the noun *channel* has given the verb *to channel*.

• Words can change their meaning and the **register** to which they belong, and examples of this were given above. Slang words can become accepted and other words may become informal in register. Dialect words may become more widely used and archaic words may be reintroduced in the language, though often with a different

meaning. It is important to remain alert to these possible developments in the vocabulary of any text you consider.

ANALYSIS OF ENGLISH TEXTS

We will now examine two texts to outline the kind of thing you
might look out for when you are faced with the same task. One text
is early and from a printed book; the other is more modern and
informal.

Caxton's English

The first text is the beginning of Caxton's prologue to his second
edition of Chaucer's *Canterbury Tales*, probably printed in 1482 at
Westminster. We reproduce it here as it occurs in the original print.

Prohemye
GRete thankes lawde and honour/ ought to be gyuen vnto the clerkes/ poetes/ and historiographs
that haue wreton many noble bokes of wysedom
of the lyues/ passiõs/ & myracles of holy sayntes
of hystoryes/ of noble and famous Actes/ and   5
faittes/ And of the cronycles sith the begynnyng

of the creacion of the world/ vnto thys present tyme/ by whyche
we ben dayly enformed/ and haue knowleche of many thynges/
of whom we sheld not haue knowen/ yf they had not left to vs
theyr monumentis wreton/ Emong whom and inespecial to fore   10
alle other we ought to gyue a synguler laude vnto that noble &
grete philosopher Gefferey chaucer the whiche for his ornate wry-
tyng in our tongue may wel haue the name of a laureate poe-
te/ For to fore that he by hys labour enbelysshyd/ ornated/ and
made faire our englisshe/ in thys Royame was had rude speche &   15
incongrue/ as yet it appiereth by olde bookes/ whyche at thys day
ought not to haue place ne be compared emõg ne to hys beauteuous volumes/ and aournate writynges/

• The first thing to notice is the **genre** to which this text belongs. It is
a prologue to a printed book, what today would be a preface. A
preface uses inflated language because it both promotes the book
and offers thanks to those who have helped in its production. It uses
the inflated language of praise often with many nouns and
adjectives. Even today you might expect phrases like 'generous
and unstinting support' and 'learned and astute advice' to occur

in prefaces. The vocabulary is likely to be Latinate and learned; the sentences long and somewhat involved. An informal note is not usually struck. We expect the same to be true of Caxton's passage; the language is indeed formal, not to say pompous. It is this aspect which might need most comment, though naturally as a text written at the end of the fifteenth century there are other characteristics which apply to most texts then.

• The **punctuation** and **spelling** are of their time. The only punctuation mark is the slash (/) which acts as both full stop and comma. What might be regarded as the start of sentences have capitals, though capitals are also used elsewhere in a system which is not very clear. Some word division is not in accord with modern practice and there are abbreviations, both the macron (-) representing *n* or *m* (*passiõs* = *passions*, etc.) and the ampersand (&) representing *and*. The surname *chaucer* and the name of the language *englisshe* do not have capital letters.

The spelling exhibits variation both in the text and as compared with modern English. We have the pairs *lawde/laude*, *hys/his* and *wrytyng/writynges*. The plural of nouns can be spelt *-es* or *-is*. Of the many words which are spelt differently today we may note the following (with the modern form in brackets): *grete* (*great*), *wreton* (*written*), *bokes* (*books*), *wysedom* (*wisdom*), *faittes* (*feats*), *creacion* (*creation*), *knowleche* (*knowledge*), *enbelysshyd* (*embellished*), *royame* (*realm*) and *appiereth* (*appears*). These spellings are not untypical of their time and do not represent anything unusual for fifteenth-century printers, who were a little more cavalier in their attitude to spelling than some of their contemporaries.

Some spellings also represent the state of English spelling at the time. Thus *u* and *v* are used in different ways from what we are accustomed to today, for now the former is a vowel and the latter a consonant. In the fifteenth century *u/v* were distinguished by their position in a word and not by their function as sounds. So *v* occurs at the beginning of a word and *u* occurs inside a word, no matter whether the sound intended was a vowel or consonant. Thus *v* occurs in *vs* (a vowel) and *volumes* (a consonant), and *u* occurs in *haue* (a consonant) and *volumes* (a vowel). Neither usually occurs at the end of a word.

• It is not possible to use the spellings to decide what the **sounds** of fifteenth-century English may have been like. The spelling *emong* (l.10) with initial *e-* does not indicate a different pronunciation from *among.* Equally we cannot assume that the initial morphemes in *enbelysshyd* (l. 14) and *incongrue* (l. 16) were pronounced differently. The spelling *emong* had varied for many years with *among* and the choice between them was now arbitrary. The distinction between *in-* and *en-* was partly based on the origin of the form from Latin or French, but the two spellings had become interchangeable and not significant as far as sound is concerned.

• As for morphology there are a couple of verb inflections which are notable, though both are regular in the fifteenth century. The third person singular of the present indicative could end in *-eth* or *-es,* and in *appiereth* (l. 16) we have an *-eth* ending where today we would expect *appears.* Both forms could be found in the fifteenth century, but the *-eth* one may have been regarded as a little more old fashioned and elevated, and so it is hardly surprising that Caxton should use it in a passage like this. The other verb form worth comment is *we ben* (l. 8) which not only has the older form *be-,* but also the older inflection *-n.* This was by the fifteenth century largely confined to one or two special verbs like the verb *to be.* This form was being replaced in the fifteenth century, though it was by no means archaic yet. Again it may have been chosen for stylistic reasons. With regard to the plural of nouns and pronouns we can notice that *other* (l. 11) is here a plural, though today we would have *others.* This *s*-less plural is historical and survives from the original declension of this word in Old English.

• The **organisation** of sentences and their **word order** are what one might expect from a preface at this time. A preface needs a formal style and this can be achieved by arranging words, phrases and clauses in groups of twos and threes. We can notice in the first sentence such groups as *thankes lawde and honour, clerkes/ poetes/ and historiographs,* and *lyues/ passiōs/ & myracles.* The organisation of the first sentence is such that it is difficult to know exactly where it finishes, and the absence of full stops makes it particularly trouble-some in this case. The precise links in the structure are not what we would expect today. Thus *noble bokes of wysedom of the lyues* suggests books containing wisdom from the lives, etc. of saints. Then *of hystoryes/ of noble and famous. Actes* presumably refers back to books, i.e. they have written books containing histories dealing with noble and famous deeds. But *And of the cronycles* fits in awkwardly. It can hardly start a new sentence despite the capital *A* of *And* which follows the slash after *faittes*. Probably we are to understand *bokes . . . of the cronycles*, though the introduction of *the* makes this final part of the parallel structure echo *the lyues* rather than *hystoryes*. The presence or absence of the definite article was rather less regulated in the fifteenth century than today. The whole may be understood as organised in the following manner:

noble bokes of wysedome of the lyues . . .
of hystoryes . . .
And of the cronycles . . .

However, the sentence carries on because *cronycles* is itself expanded by a very long postmodifier. But this postmodifier is not without ambiguity. It reads 'sith the begynnyng of the creacion of the world/ vnto thys present tyme/ by whyche we ben dayly enformed/ and haue knowleche of many thynges/ of whom we shold not haue knowen/ yf they had not left to vs theyr monumentis wreton'. The problem arises because Caxton has used both *by whyche* and *of whom*. *Which* could be used of both animate (cf. l. 12) and inanimate antecedents then, though today we confine it to inanimates. *Who/whom* was usually used to refer to animates, but it could be used of inanimates as well, though it was not frequently used at this time anyway. *Whyche* may be understood to refer to the *cronycles*, and *whom* could refer to *thynges, the cronycles* or even to the people who did the things which appeared in the chronicles to which Caxton refers. The last of these alternatives may seem appropriate because Caxton does introduce pronouns which have implicit rather than explicit antecedents. Thus *they* (l. 9) and *theyr* (l. 10) refer to the writers of chronicles and histories, although they have not been mentioned as such before. The next sentence starts with *Emong whom*, which refers to the writers of histories. Although today this would suggest a continuation of the postmodifier, in the fifteenth century *whom* acted as a connecting device across sentences with the sense in this instance of 'among these' and so it is better to assume that a new sentence begins here.

• There are one or two noteworthy features of word order in the passage. Standard **word order** today is subject–verb–object (**SVO**). In earlier periods of English this word order could be altered if an adverb or adverbial phrase came first in the sentence to produce adverb–verb–subject (object) (**AVS(O)**). An example of this occurs in l. 15 *in thys Royame was had rude speche*, in which the subject is *rude speche*, the verb is *was had*, and the initial adverb of place is *in this Royame*. In fact the subject is actually *rude speche & incongrue*, which exhibits another feature of word order. The two adjectives describing *speche* have been split so that one is a premodifier and the other a postmodifier. Today we would expect the order *rude & incongrue speche*, though an attempt to raise the stylistic level might allow the other order even now.

The position of adjectives was a little freer then, for although their normal position was in the premodifier position they could for stylistic reasons be found in the postmodifier slot. In l. 10 *theyr monumentis wreton* is presumably to be understood as 'their written monuments'. But in ll. 13–14 it is interesting to note that Caxton has *laureate poete* whereas we today speak of the *poet laureate*. The position of adverbs and adverbial phrases was also much freer then than now. Today we would not usually place an adverbial phrase between the subject and its verb so that an utterance like 'He in the morning catches the bus' is no longer acceptable. But there are examples of this structure in Caxton's prologue: *he by hys labour enbelysshyd* (l.14) and *whyche at thys day ought not* (ll.16–17). One final aspect of word order may be noted. In ll. 9–10 we find *yf they had not left to vs theyr monumentis wreton*. Here the indirect object *to vs* comes before the direct object *theyr monumentis wreton*. In modern English when the indirect object comes before the direct object it normally has no *to*: 'Give me the book'; it is only when it follows the direct object that the indirect one takes *to*: 'Give the book to me'. This regularisation had not been achieved yet.

• A few smaller points merit mention. The use of the relative pronoun *which* to refer to animate antecedents has already been referred to, but it does need to be noted that this pronoun can take the form *the which*; at l. 12 *the whiche*, meaning 'who', refers to Chaucer. It is not certain where this form came from, but it is sometimes thought it may have been influenced by French *lequel*. When a relative pronoun is governed by a preposition, today we tend to put the preposition at the end of the clause though we are often encouraged by stylists to put it at the front. In *of whom we shold not haue knowen* (l. 9) we find it before the relative pronoun, though in modern English it would be commoner to use 'have known of'.

The occurrence of a dummy subject *it* appears in l. 16, where it implies what has been written in the previous clause; in modern

English the subject would be understood. In earlier English conjunctions were often formed from prepositions or other parts of speech by the addition of *that* so that there is a distinction between *to fore* (l. 10, preposition) and *to fore that* (l. 14, conjunction). The use of *that* becomes less common in these conditions in the seventeenth century, although we still use it in modern English after forms like *seeing (that)* or *in view of the fact (that)*.

When a negative occurs there is a tendency to put other coordinating words in associated clauses into the negative form so that at l. 17 we have *ought not to haue place ne be compared emōg ne to hys....* The avoidance today of double or triple negation encourages us to write this as 'ought not to be given room or to be compared together with or to his...'. Notice also that Caxton has kept the old negative form *ne* which was now on its way out and was retained largely in sequences of negative forms like this one. Among the verb forms there are many auxiliaries which indicates a lofty style. In ll. 1–2 Caxton uses the passive *ought to be gyuen*, but by l. 11 he resorts to more natural *we ought to gyue*. The passive is almost always a sign of literary language and high style; notice also his use of *be compared* (l. 17). The use of *to be* as an auxiliary *to have* in *was had* (l. 15) is both characteristic of the time and a marker of an elevated style.

• There is little to record on **word-formation** in this passage. Most of the literary words are borrowed from other languages as we shall see in a minute rather than invented through the use of compounds. Similarly the unusual prefixes and suffixes are largely the result of foreign borrowing. He varies *ornated* (l. 14) with *aournate* (l. 18); and he uses *incongrue* (l. 16) and *beauteuous* (ll. 17–18) where we would have *incongruous* and *beautiful*. The word *historiographs* (l. 2) could be said to lack the final morpheme *-er*, for the usual form is *historiographers*. All of these forms are borrowed from French.

• As already indicated the **vocabulary** is affected by the wish to make the preface sound elevated and literary. There is consequently a large number of words borrowed from Latin and particularly French, though it does not mean that Caxton was the first to introduce them into English. This is an original composition rather than a translation in which one expects to find many words borrowed from the original and so new to the language. The vocabulary is not notable for its new words so much as for a constant attempt to use **learned** and **abstract** words of Latin origin rather than simple words of Anglo–Saxon origin. This often means repeating some words of praise: *grete* occurs twice, *lawde* twice, *noble* three times and *ornate* twice as an adjective and once as a verb. There is a superfluity of nouns and adjectives, and some verbs are made up of *have* or *make* plus a noun or adjective: *haue knowleche* (l. 8), *made faire* (l. 15), *haue place* (l. 17).

• Although a few words are now obsolete, whatever difficulties of understanding this passage contains today arise more from **changes of meaning** than from obsolesence of words. *Lawde* (l. 1), *faittes* (l. 6), *historiographs* (l. 2), and *sith* (l. 6) are now obsolete, but consider the many words that are now familiar in a different sense. A *clerk* (l. 2) is now an office worker who does such jobs as filing and not an educated person, often in holy orders, who writes learned books; a *passion* (l. 4) is now only infrequently the suffering of intense pain associated with Christ and more often the overflow of powerful emotions associated particularly with sexual attraction. *Actes* (l. 5) would now usually be referred to as 'deeds'; *faittes* (l. 6) if it survives is spelt *feats*, but is archaic. *Monumentis* (l. 10) would not normally now be used of written texts in book form since it refers to large public memorials made of stone or similar materials. *Synguler* (l. 11) here means 'particular, special' rather than 'unusual'. We are hardly likely to use the word *philosopher* (l. 12) of Chaucer, which here means 'a writer of moral and uplifting works'. *Ornate* (l. 12) might be used of style rather than writing in general. *Tongue* (l. 13) and *speche* (l. 15) have become specialised in meaning; they no longer refer to language as a whole. *Rude* (l. 15) now means 'vulgar' rather than more generally inelegant and unsophisticated, and *incongrue* (l. 16, 'incongruous') would not be used to mean the same as 'inelegant' although the sense of 'ludicrously inappropriate' is inevitably always present.

• Some words are now **archaic** or **specialised**. *Royame* (l. 15, for 'realm') has fallen into disuse except with some writers for a specialised sense to evoke the past or patriotism. A word like *cronycles* (l. 6) survives only in a technical sense. We do not use *ornate* (l. 14) as a verb and we do not use the form *aournate* any more.

This passage is particularly characteristic for its vocabulary and syntax which are motivated by the genre to which it belongs. Within its genre the text is not unusual for its time. Most of the features

which are noted here could readily be parallelled by other contemporary texts. Caxton was not trying to be innovative or unusual;
he was trying to imitate the style of what he considered to be the
fashionable writers of his time and the preceding age, one of whom
was of course Chaucer.

William Clift's English

The second example comes from the end of the eighteenth century;
it is a letter sent by William Clift on 1 July 1797 to his sister
Elizabeth. William was a member of the Clift family of Bodmin in
Cornwall. The youngest son of a Cornish miller, he went to London
where he became an apprentice to the founder of modern British
surgery, John Hunter (1728–93). William became the first Conser-
vator of the Hunterian Museum of anatomical specimens, which is
now housed in Lincoln's Inn Fields, where the Royal College of
Surgeons of England was built to house it. Five of William's siblings
lived to become adults and the six of them corresponded with one
another. Although William went to London the other children
mostly remained in the West Country, though Robert joined the
navy. The level of education that each received varied as does their
command of Standard English. Not unnaturally William's English
approximates most closely to the Standard English of the time and
one of his letters is reproduced here from *The Clift Family Correspondence 1792–1846*, edited by Frances Austin (Sheffield: Centre for
English Cultural Tradition and Language, 1991), p. 155.

Dear Sister
  And I hope as worthy to be called so as ever; I received a
letter yesterday and I should have wrote by the return of post
if I had not been so much astonished at its contents. I must say
I was astonished very much and more so the longer I look at it,
and that I thought it would require some longer time than an   5
hour or two to take into consideration the different charges
that are there brought against me tho' I must beg leave to say
as undeservedly and more so than you who complain as I
believe I shall make appear pretty plainly before I have done, –
And first, for I shall follow your letter – You desire to know   10
wherein you have offended me and did not expect at one time
to have been so slighted – I could almost send back the same
words – I find you yourself do not say you have ever wrote to

me since you received my letter at Linkinhorn for if you had
wrote, & with the same direction as you used to put I do not   15
doubt but I should have got it, and I here declare I have never
received any letter from you since that informing me of your
journey to Linkinhorn nor did I know you had left that place
till yesterday when I read your letter. I received a letter from
sister Joanna dated 27th March 97, desiring much to know if I   20
had heard from you and testified a great surprize at hearing
that you was in Penzance, and that being all she said, I
concluded she did not know how to direct to you nor did I
then suppose you was there, but that she had been wrong
inform'd, and in my answer to her I complained smartly of   25
your neglect and which she can answer for me if ever you
write to her, and when Mr & Mrs Gilbert were in town about
two months ago, they could only inform me that they had
heard you was in Penzance, and when I told her I was very
uneasy at not hearing from you she said she dare say you were   30
well and was unwilling to put me to expence for she knew, she
said, that you was very considerate, but I beg no such
consideration may be an excuse for neglect in future.

• It is important to remember firstly the **genre** – that this is a letter,
which is naturally somewhat informal as it is to a member of the
family, and secondly that it was written just before 1800, by which
time the standard language had been the subject of many books and
grammars, and a large number of dictionaries including the one by
Dr Johnson had been produced. Since the letter writer is educated
and lived in London one anticipates that it would reflect standard
usage of his day or perhaps one might say the informal standard of
his day.

• Spelling and morphology were by now fairly well regulated. The
informal genre of letter writing allows abbreviations such as *tho'*,
inform'd and the ampersand (&), and these are abbreviations which
might well occur in letters today. The ending -'*d* is not used
frequently, for the expanded -*ed* form is more regular. The letter's
spelling is standard though some variation was still accepted.
William uses *surprize* (l. 21) and *expence* (l. 31), which could perhaps
still be found in letters today though the standard forms are *surprise*
and *expense*.

• The **punctuation** in this letter is light, though as compared with the Caxton passage it uses modern punctuation marks, the semi-colon, the comma, the full stop and the dash. The sentences appear to go on and on because they are not very tightly structured, and the light punctuation reinforces this impression. The second half of the passage (ll. 19–33) is written as a single sentence, but it contains many ideas which might have been more clearly expressed in separate sentences. One may in part attribute this to the informality of a letter, where a writer puts his thoughts down without troubling himself too much about their organisation into sentences. Sometimes the use of dashes appears illogical. At l. 10 the *And first* goes with *You desire to know*, because it refers to the first query in Elizabeth's letter which he is going to answer. But they are separated by a dash and the *You* has a capital as though it was introducing a new sentence. But it must be said that although the punctuation does not always conform to the standardised rules, the letter is perfectly intelligible.

• Inevitably most comment on texts written within the last two to three hundred years is likely to focus on points of **grammar, syntax** and **vocabulary**. In this passage one may notice that the past participle of *write* is *wrote*, not once but regularly. There is an interesting use of *was* with the pronoun *you*, though once the form used is *were*. It seems as though *you was* was William's usual form in the letter, but he used *you were* to indicate something hypothetical, as though he was employing the old subjunctive. Consider the utterance at l. 30: *she said she dare say you were well and was unwilling*. Here we may assume *you were well* is hypothetical (i.e. she assumed and hoped you were well, although she did not know for certain), but *[you] was unwilling to put me to expence* is a fact because Mrs Gilbert knew that was part of Elizabeth's character. It is noteworthy that even at this time an educated man writing from London could use forms that one would have assumed had been banished from the standard language long since. Although the letter may be informal, it does not create the impression of talking down to less educated people.

Another point worth comment is that in English many adverbs originate from adjectives and by the sixteenth century both had the same form. In order to distinguish one from the other the ending *-ly* was increasingly added to the adverb form and this was encouraged by grammarians. But even today not all adverbs have this *-ly* ending (one can *drive slow* or *drive slowly*), but most do. In William's letter most adverbs do have *-ly* (*undeservedly* l. 8, *plainly* l. 9, *smartly* l. 25) but one still has the old form without *-ly*, *wrong inform'd* (l. 24) where today we would have *wrongly*. With regard to adverbs one may also note that *much* is now largely obsolete as an adverb except in negative contexts so that *I was astonished very much* (l. 4) and *desiring much* (l. 20) now strike us as odd. But even *I had not been so much astonished* (l. 3) appears strange since today *much* usually follows directly on *not* to mean 'a little' rather than as here to indicate a large amount.

• The **word order** in the letter is much as one would expect today except for the use of *nor* as a conjunction followed by inversion of the subject and auxiliary: *nor did I know* (l. 18) and *nor did I then suppose* (l. 23).

The informality of a letter allows for a certain ellipsis or leaving out words which have to be understood and this often produces possible ambiguity. In the passage already commented on, *she said she dare say you were well and was unwilling*, the absence of *you* before *was unwilling* might lead modern readers to assume that the subject of *was unwilling* was *she* rather than *you*. The first sentence of the letter is very elliptical, *And I hope as worthy to be called so as ever*. This follows on from the address *Dear Sister* and the way William introduces the letter with *And* indicates that he still had *Dear Sister* in mind, for it is otherwise very unusual to start any text with *And*. The sense must be something like 'And I hope you are still worthy to be called "Dear Sister" as you have always been in the past'. It is a mild rebuke on his part at the receipt of a letter which he clearly considered to be less than friendly. Indeed, many of his sentences have the same type of elliptical expression. In l. 4 we find *and more so the longer I look at it*, meaning 'the more I look at the letter the more astonished I am at its contents'. In this particular case the use of *look* indicates that although the rest of the letter is in the past tense (*I was astonished . . . I thought*) he wishes to indicate that his looking continues from the receipt of the letter to the time of his writing his own.

• The way in which **clauses are linked** is worth comment. In William's *You desire to know wherein you have offended me and did not expect at one time to have been so slighted* (ll. 10–12), the second clause starting *did not* must have *you* as its subject. But it must be a main clause parallel to *You desire* and not a subordinate clause parallel to *you have offended*, which is what at first seems to be the case. We noticed in the Caxton prologue that *that* was used where we would not find it today, and the same is true of this passage and we may assume that this type of construction lasted longer in informal writing than it did in more formal prose. In the sentence *I must say I was astonished . . . and that I thought* (ll. 3–5), the precise role of *that* is uncertain. It may be simply added to the co-ordinate conjunction *and* to strengthen it or it may indicate the introduction of a subordinate clause dependent upon *I must say*, even though the first subordinate clause *I was astonished* is not introduced by *that*. The first possibility may appear to be suggested by the example *but that* in the sentence *I concluded she did not know . . . but that she had been wrong inform'd* (ll. 22–24), where the second clause seems to be dependent upon *I concluded*.

Immediately before these clauses there is a different use of *that* in *and that being all she said* (l. 22), because the sense of that clause is 'as that was all she said'. The use of *which* at l. 26 is as a general connective referring to all that is mentioned in the previous part of the letter; it has the sense 'all of this'. This use was permissible in formal prose at an earlier date, but gradually came to be more characteristic of informal writing such as letters.

• There are a few examples of **determiner** which are different from today. The use of *a letter* (ll. 1–2) rather than *your letter* strikes a cold and distant note. Today we would probably write *by return of post* rather than *by the return of post* because the expression has become somewhat idiomatic, but here may not have achieved that status. The expression *some longer time* is unusual since today we would probably simply have *more*. Even at its time the use of *some* at all is somewhat heavy. The relative pronouns are more or less in accord with modern practice, though William uses *wherein* (l. 11) where we might have preferred *how* or *in what*.

• The most interesting feature of the vocabulary is its rather elevated tone. A large number of the words are of Latin origin and the effect is one of some formality although the letter is otherwise informal. There are no slang or unconventional expressions, though there are some more idiomatic ones like *pretty plainly* (l. 9) and *smartly* (l. 25), here with the sense of 'promptly, pointedly'.

The vocabulary is that of an educated man, even though the syntax is more appropriate to a more informal genre. Consider the following expressions: *astonished at its contents* (l. 3) instead of 'surprised at what it said' with the use of the noun *contents* instead of a verb phrase giving a heavy tone; *take into consideration* (l. 6) instead of 'consider, weigh'; *the different charges* (l. 6) which has a legal flavour found elsewhere in the letter instead of just 'the points'; *undeservedly* (l. 8) instead of 'without cause'; *desire* (l. 10 and elsewhere) instead of 'wish'; *declare* (l. 16 with its legal overtones); *testified a great surprize* (l. 21) rather than 'was surprised'; and many others.

It is not surprising that most of the words used in the letter are still found in the language though some have changed their meaning. *Direction* (l. 15) for 'address' and *how to direct to you* (l. 23) for 'your address' have fallen out of use in these meanings. The expression *direction as you used to put* (l. 15) has other features that need comment. The use of *as* for *which* was common in formal English at an earlier period, but has tended since then to become informal. The expression *you used to put* meaning literally 'you were accustomed to put on the letter' would now be perhaps 'you have always used'. The use of *sister* (l. 20) as a term of address rather as we still use *uncle* or *aunt* is now obsolete.

These are some of the features in the language of this passage which reflect both its genre and the period at which it was written. It is important to remember both of these aspects in looking at any passage.

EXERCISES

In this section we include two passages for linguistic analysis so that you can see how far the language in them differs from modern English and how far it represents that of their genres from the time at which they were written. There are also some questions about the history of English which could form the basis for class work and discussion.

John Hart's English

The first passage is from John Hart's *Orthographie* published in 1569. John Hart was interested in spelling reform and his book contains comments on the faults of contemporary spelling, how English sounds are made, and a new spelling system, for which examples are also provided. This extract reproduced from the original edition comments upon some of the inadequacies of the spelling of his time and the defence that some have offered for it.

NOwe before I open the particular vices and abuse in our English writing, I will recite the chiefest of thobiections, which my contraries vse. Some of them bring forth such smal reasons (worse than Corinths) as it were but labor lost to write them.

But others there are which maintaine our superfluitie of letters in writing with foure arguments, wherein is some likelyhode of reason.

The first is vnder pretence to shew the deriuation and spring of some wordes borowed or taken forth of strange tongues.

Another is, that it should be lawfull to abuse some letters to put a difference betwixt equiuoces or wordes of one sounde.

The thirde is for the time of vowels.

But their strongest defence (which comprehendeth all) and that wherin they most triumph, is vse, wherof I will first speake generallye vntill I haue occasion by the perticulars. As I haue communed with some of them, first like friendes they would perswade me, not to speake of any misuse in our English writing, which (they saye) is of late brought to such a perfection as neuer the lyke was before. Yet I stayed not therewith fro my purpose, but woulde aunswere them partly with the reasons in my Preface. Then would they further replie, the power and soundes of some letters, haue bene ouer long double, for nowe to be receyued single, whatsoeuer they were aunciently: for that which vse by little and little and with long continuance bringeth into any peoples maner of doings, is neuer spoken or written against without great offence to the multitude: which will be ten folde more stiffenecked to receyue any newe letters, than a teame of wilde Steeres would be at first to receyue the bearing of their yokes.

Samuel Johnson's English

The second passage is from the work of that famous lexicographer, Samuel Johnson. In 1747 he published his plan for a dictionary as a prelude to starting his own dictionary which was eventually published in 1755. Some of the views he expressed in his plan he was forced to change as he worked on the dictionary itself. In the passage provided here, reproduced from the original edition, Johnson comments on the matter of spelling, although he arrives at different conclusions from those of Hart.

WHEN all the words are selected and arranged, the first part of the work to be considered is the ORTHOGRAPHY, which was long vague and uncertain, which at last, when its fluctuation ceased, was in many cases settled but by accident, and in which, according to your Lordship's observation, there is still great uncertainty among the best critics; nor is it easy to state a rule by which we may decide between custom and reason, or between the equiponderant authorities of writers alike eminent for judgment and accuracy.

The great orthographical contest has long subsisted between etymology and pronunciation. It has been demanded, on one hand, that men should write as they speak; but as it has been shewn that this conformity never was attained in any language, and that it is not more easy to perswade men to agree exactly in speaking than in writing, it may be asked with equal propriety, why men do not rather speak as they write. In France, where this controversy was at its greatest height, neither party, however ardent, durst adhere steadily to their own rule; the etymologist was often forced to spell with the people; and the advocate for the authority of pronunciation, found it sometimes deviating so capriciously from the received use of writing, that he was constrained to comply with the rule of his adversaries, lest he should loose the end by the means, and be left alone by following the croud.

WHEN a question of orthography is dubious, that practice has, in my opinion, a claim to preference, which preserves the greatest number of radical letters, or seems most to comply with the general custom of our language. But the chief rule which I propose to follow, is to make no innovation, without a reason sufficient to balance the inconvenience of change; and such reasons I do not expect often to find. All change is of itself an evil, which ought not to be hazarded but for evident advantage; and as inconstancy is in every case a mark of weakness, it will add nothing to the reputation of our tongue.

ESSAY QUESTIONS

Here are some questions for essay writing or class discussion.

1 The sixteenth century witnessed what is known as the 'ink-horn controversy'. What is meant by this term and why did people at the time indulge in ink-horn terms?

2 Why is the technical vocabulary of English largely based on the classical languages?

3 What influence did the foundation of the Royal Society have upon the development of English?

4 Why is there no academy in England to regulate the language?'

5 Many in the eighteenth century wanted to 'fix' the language. What did they mean by this and to what extent did their efforts fail?

6 Illustrate some of the rules of grammar proposed by the eighteenth-century grammarians and discuss what motives prompted these rules.

7 Comment on the principles Dr Johnson followed in writing his dictionary.

8 Illustrate some of the ways in which French has influenced the development of English.

9 What effect did the British Empire have on English vocabulary?

10 Comment on the interaction of standard and non-standard varieties in any one period of English.

4

Language Variety and the Social Context

LANGUAGE AS AN ARBITRARY SYSTEM

Before we consider language variety we need to be aware of the nature of human languages.

• Language is an arbitrary system of signs, by which we can understand for the present purpose that there is no inherent connection between the words we use and the things to which they refer. We English may refer to the canine domestic pet as *dog*, the French as *chien*, and the Germans as *Hund*. There is nothing in any of these words which makes such a meaning predictable or inevitable, and to that extent the arrangement of sounds which form the word *dog* is purely arbitrary in its reference to the canine quadruped. If we all agreed that this animal should be called *blump* in English, that word would be the one we used and would be just as arbitrary in its significance as *dog*. Our choice of the word *dog* is related to the historical development of the language, but that does not make its use any less arbitrary.

The organisation of words into sequences to make up phrases or clauses is equally arbitrary; though we may talk about grammatical rules, these simply represent a **codification** of what actually happens in the language and are not an explanation of or justification for what happens. In English we normally put an adjective before a noun so that we say *a happy man* rather than *a man happy*. In French the reverse is the case. There is nothing good or bad about one order as compared with the other; they are just different and they are both equally arbitrary.

• Naturally in order to make ourselves intelligible in a language we follow the **conventions** of that language: if we used strange words or an unusual order people would assume we were either foreigners or mad. But we can and do exploit the arbitrary quality of language.

80

Because there is no inherent connection between the word *dog* and the animal it represents, we can refer to it by using other names. If there was an inherent link between *dog* and the canine pet, then there would be no room for any other word to refer to it. But a dog can be called *hound* (usually in a semi-jocular way) and it can be called *woof-woof* (usually in children's language). These words too are arbitrary. Some readers might assume that there is a link between *woof-woof* and the domestic canine because the word is onomatopoeic, that is, it reproduces the noise a dog makes when barking. Up to a point this is true, but its truth is more apparent than real. If *woof-woof* is the noise that dogs make when barking, one would expect all languages to represent that action by the same combination of sounds. This does not happen because each language represents the noise a dog makes when barking in a different way, a way that bears some resemblance to that noise but is otherwise fairly arbitrary. We English assume that dogs actually say *woof-woof* when barking because that is the word we have chosen to represent their barking onomatopoeically: what we hear is what our own word has taught us to expect.

• It is the arbitrary nature of the system which allows us as speakers to feed into any language our attitudes towards particular words, usages and varieties. **Fashion** and **prejudice** are very much a part of language, and they reflect social attitudes and ideals. This can be seen in an area such as taboo words. What may be regarded as taboo changes from one generation to another and from one society to another. Today in England death is much more of a taboo subject than sex, though fifty years ago the reverse was true. Consequently many people find it impolite to use the words *to die* and *dead*, preferring to use a euphemism, i.e. a round-about and possibly metaphorical way of saying the same thing. Hence people might say of someone that she *has passed away* or *gone over* rather than simply saying she *has died*. We will make certain assumptions about people according to our own attitudes and to prevailing social mores depending upon which of these forms they use. Hence if someone used the expression *she has died* we might regard him as a little brusque; if he said *she has passed away* we might regard him as sensitive to the taboo around death; and if he said *she has gone over* we might assume that he used a language which verged on the precious. Our assumptions would be based on our own social background and age: a younger person might think *she has died* was the only appropriate expression, whereas an older person would regard *she has gone over* as the norm. The range of reactions to these expressions can be extensive, even though it is possible to make some generalisations about expected ones.

STANDARDISATION AND PRESCRIPTIVISM

The history of English shows that there have been regional dialects since the Anglo–Saxons arrived in this country. Although speakers in the past clearly recognised differences in dialect, it is difficult to know how the speaker of one dialect responded to the speech of a speaker from a different dialect area. Inevitably differences in speech (like differences in other social habits such as clothes and eating styles) are likely to be a cause of surprise and of amusement. Sometimes if the speakers of one dialect are considered socially superior for one reason or another, the surprise may be mingled with envy and respect. But within writing and literature differences are most often introduced to represent people who are socially inferior and thus a matter for comedy. As early as Chaucer's *The Canterbury Tales* we find that in the Reeve's Tale the two Cambridge undergraduates are said to come from 'far in the North' and are given speech forms which represent a northern dialect. It cannot be claimed that the London dialect was by then so well established as the socially superior form of English that the use of the northern dialect was a way of indicating the undergraduates' social standing. But the difference between their speech and that of the other characters is unmistakable.

• From the fifteenth century the London dialect was used as the basis for standard written English, and it is important to emphasise *written* in this connexion. In particular standardisation affects **spelling** which was gradually standardised through the work of printers and the makers of dictionaries. It is because modern English spelling is so rigid that people can complain about how many others cannot spell properly.

The notion of what is right and what is wrong is much easier to defend in the case of spelling, since spelling is the one feature of language which can easily be regulated. **Vocabulary** continues to change in any language, and although there are attempts to establish boundaries between words which are acceptable and those which are not, those boundaries are in a constant state of flux. New words are added to the language and words which yesterday were socially unacceptable are today permitted and common. In Shaw's *Pygmalion* Eliza could cause a stir by saying 'Not bloody likely', but such an expression today if uttered by a young woman of social standing would hardly arouse much comment. Dictionaries contain words which are usually found in the written language and which are meant as a descriptive account of the vocabulary. Some people assume that dictionaries include only the acceptable words in the language and that words not in the dictionary are somehow not proper English words. However, dictionaries are continually updated to include new words and the dictionary makers themselves are now more liberal in their policies of what words to include in a dictionary, particularly in regard to the spoken language.

Judgements about an individual's vocabulary are now likely to be based on the overall level of the words used rather than on single words. Words in a different grammatical context are as likely to be noticed as new words or words from a different register. Thus many speakers use *notice* as a transitive verb only (i.e. with an object: 'They noticed the vase on the table'), whereas others use it as an intransitive verb as well (i.e. without an object: 'It notices' with the sense 'It shows'). Those who use the verb as transitive only will be struck by the other usage and think it strange because they will not be able to explain why it is used in this way. But a new word or an unfamiliar word used by a particular group or class will be identified in some way, perhaps as an Americanism or as a teenage word for example, and will be judged according to the listener's social values.

Syntax was more regulated from the eighteenth century when grammarians produced a list of rules (a list of do's and don't's) for the language, which were incorporated into the grammar books used in schools. Although some of these rules never became fully accepted, most did as far as written.English is concerned and so established a basis by which people's command of English could be judged. Spelling and grammar, and to a lesser extent vocabulary, became part of the educational programme from the nineteenth century onwards and it soon became the mark of an educated person that he could spell correctly and write grammatically. It followed that those who could not achieve the approved standard were regarded as uneducated and since education is often unwisely correlated with intelligence, those who could not spell or write grammatically were considered both uneducated and stupid. From that position certain attitudes towards them could easily develop. Today approaches towards grammar are more relaxed, but spelling is still regarded by many as a shibboleth even though 'incorrect' spelling is commonly found – in formal correspondence, in government documents and in all types of printed material.

• The position in English is slightly complicated by the fact that there has never been in England an academy like the Academie Française in France to lay down rules for spelling or grammar which had the force of law. If some aspects of language are regarded as 'correct' and some others as 'incorrect', it is because certain people, whether teachers or government ministers, describe them as such although they have no particular authority for their pronouncements. As a consequence attitudes to language are rather flexible and subject to fashion and prejudice. What is acceptable today was not acceptable yesterday; but it is sometimes very difficult to find out what is acceptable. Different people have different views on the matter, and this only accentuates the unease which many people, certainly the less well educated who want to be considered socially acceptable, have towards their own language.

• With **speech** the position has been different because the problems of encouraging a uniform spoken variety are much greater than those for standardising writing. As already indicated, differences at a spoken level were noted from an early stage in the language, which is hardly surprising for we all speak the language but not all of us write or read it. Some of the attitudes to variation in speech can be traced in literary texts. In Elizabethan and Jacobean plays there is a stage rustic dialect based on the pronunciation characteristic of southern and particularly south-western speakers. When in *King Lear* Edgar adopts a disguise as a poor peasant Shakespeare provides him with a language which is quite different from the normal language of the play for it represents this stage dialect:

> Good gentleman, go your gait, and let poor volk pass. And 'chud ha' bin zwagger'd out of my life, 'twould not ha' bin zo long as 'tis by a vortnight. Nay, come not near th'old man; keep out, che vor' ye, or ise try whither your costard or my ballow be the harder. Chill be plain with you. (IV.6.234–9)

Some spellings indicate a different pronunciation, *volk* for *folk*, and the vocabulary is also non-standard, *costard* and *ballow*. At a still later period Cockney was often used in novels, such as those by Dickens, to represent speech forms different from the standard, though Cockney speakers are often represented as quick-witted rather than as dull.

• Although education did encourage particular **pronunciations**, before the advent of the radio and tape recorders it was difficult to promulgate preferred pronunciations through writing because not everyone could interpret the written form to produce the approved pronunciation. This remains a problem in dictionaries which do not use the International Phonetic Alphabet (IPA) for their guide to the pronunciation of words, because readers may still find difficulty in achieving the correct interpretation of the symbols used. With the development of radio and television it is possible for everyone to hear Received Pronunciation, that form of spoken English which conforms most closely to the approved form of the spoken language just as Standard English does in the written language.

In the early days of radio broadcasting there was some emphasis on all announcers conforming to a single spoken form as far as possible. But this ideal was never achieved and it has long since ceased to be an ideal. Announcers today use a wide variety of accents and varying levels of formality. While it probably remains true for broadcasting that the norms of Standard English are those which announcers are encouraged to observe, they can use different pronunciations in their speech and they can adopt certain levels of informality which might seem to ignore those norms. In chat shows and other forms of broadcasting there is even greater freedom. Furthermore, through films and satellite television it is possible to hear the voices of people from all over the world over whose English the broadcasting authorities have no control. The effect of broadcasting has been to allow people to hear many different varieties of English from all over the world. Although this has not necessarily undermined the perceived status of Received Pronunciation, it perhaps has made it appear to speakers of the language that a high degree of variety exists and that many people, even quite distinguished ones, can use forms of spoken English which differ from those in Received Pronunciation.

USER-RELATED AND USE-RELATED VARIATION

The two previous sections have considered some general character-istics of language, but it is important to remember that a distinction exists between what can be called 'user-related' and 'use-related' varieties of language.

• The difference is very close to the distinction between **dialect** and **register**. The community into which we are born, the geographical area in which that community is localised, the time at which we live and the education which we receive (whether locally or elsewhere) are all likely to affect the language we use.

Although this is particularly true of the sounds of language, it also affects the **vocabulary** and **grammar** which we employ. To some extent our user-related variety is something that comes naturally, almost subconsciously. It is true that those who are socially mobile may well try to change their user-related variety, though it is very difficult for someone to lose all traces of their original user-related variety. Naturally others take pride in their variety if it is different from the standard, because they like to exhibit their geographical affiliations. It is often easier to eradicate differences in grammar and vocabulary than it is to change one's pronunciation. For the most part each individual has one user-related variety. But each person has many use-related varieties, because the term implies adjusting one's language to the different situations in which one finds oneself on a daily basis. Dialect is usually user-related and register use-related.

• From what has been written about user-related varieties, it is clear that use-related variety exhibits itself most often in **grammar** and **vocabulary**. According to the situation in which the language used occurs, it is possible to imagine a group of people being addressed by the same person in the following ways: 'Ladies and Gentlemen', 'Comrades', 'Dear Friends', 'OK chaps', 'Hey, you lot' or 'You miserable bastards'. Equally a social occasion may dictate the use of a euphemism so that to one person you might say 'He just dropped dead', whereas to another you might prefer to phrase that as 'He passed away suddenly'.

Grammar may also change according to the social situation. For example, we may use a question rather than a command or a statement because a question is usually thought to be less forceful and more polite than a statement or a command. Consider the following three ways of saying the same thing:

1 Close the door.
2 Would you mind closing the door?
3 It would be nice if you closed the door.

There is no doubt that **1** is much more forceful than **2**, and so you might expect it to be used when a superior addresses an inferior in status, as for example a teacher to someone in the first form. The status of **3**, a statement, is less easy to determine. It could be ironic, implying that the door ought to have been closed by the addressee already, or it could be a very polite way of asking for the door to be closed. There may in use-related varieties be less change in the **phonic level** (the way the sounds are pronounced), though there may be some, particularly in matters of stress and how this affects whether sounds are run together and whether unstressed vowels are pronounced at all. At a more formal level one would say 'Give me' with the /v/ of *give* clearly pronounced and with *me* pronounced as /mi/; whereas at a less formal level one might say 'Gimmie' with no /v/ sound at all and with the *me* element pronounced as /mɪ/ or something like that.

● Attitudes to different people are likely to be influenced by whether differences in language are perceived to be user-related or use-related. In theory all people from the same community are likely to speak in a similar way depending on their level of education. People from the same geographical area are likely to use the same dialect. At all events they are likely to have the same pronunciation to a greater or lesser extent. Hence our reaction to the way that person speaks will reflect our perception of that dialect and the geographical area it comes from: he or she will to some extent conform to a type. You might, for example, think that the Birmingham pronunciation is slovenly and the Somerset pronunciation is homely and rural and you may judge the speakers who use these pronunciations in accordance with the stereotypes you have of people who come from those areas. But a failure by a speaker to observe what you consider the appropriate norms in a use-related variety may well colour your attitudes to that person's educational and social attainments.

User-related varieties

Although there is considerable overlap between user-related and use-related varieties, it is important to keep these categories separate.

• The sounds we use will be determined to a large extent by the speech community into which we were born and the education we receive, even though we may vary our speech in accordance with the social situations in which we find ourselves. The fact that we talk about 'English' as a single language means that any variety of language which we can understand we will identify as English and let our prejudices work to guide our reactions to the speaker. But it is doubtful whether certain pidgins and creoles (see below), which are simplified varieties of English developed in various language-contact situations, should be called English at all. It is characteristic of pidgins that they simplify morphology and syntax in order to make communication easier among people who have a variety of language backgrounds, so that the plural *boys* may be expressed through repetition *boy boy*. Although this is an essential procedure to assist communication in such situations, some people may well interpret the resulting simplified form of English (or English mixed with other languages) as a bastardised form of English and condemn those who speak it as illiterate or uneducated. But the majority of English speakers rarely come into contact with pidgins except perhaps through literature or the media. But we do regard all varieties which we can understand as English, though we tend to have more crystallised attitudes towards those which are better known to us.

• The varieties of English best known to us are those which are found within England as native varieties and around which various attitudes have developed over time, sometimes over centuries. It has to be said though that the average English person cannot easily distinguish among all the varieties that exist regionally. We tend to distinguish certain broad types. There are the national varieties of Scots, Welsh and Irish and then the regional varieties within England. For most people they will probably assume that they can distinguish a northern variety, a Midlands variety, and a south-western variety. In addition people will probably think they can pick out a Cockney, a Liverpudlian and perhaps one or two other

city-based varieties. Certain linguistic features have become associated with these varieties, even though they may be shared by
many dialects. Thus many may regard the dropping of initial *h*- as
characteristic of Cockney, and the pronunciation of words like *grass*
with /æ/ as typical of northern speakers.

● Attitudes towards these different varieties have become stereo-
typed and an interesting project could involve checking how far
these stereotypes are changing. If you tape a speaker of Scots, one of
Liverpudlian, one from the Somerset area and one from Newcastle,
for example, you can play the tapes to a number of listeners and ask
them to score each speaker for such things as education, honesty,
reliability, cleverness and so on. This will reveal what attitudes
particular pronunciations may evoke for some people.

Our attitude towards these speakers is to some extent moulded by
the attitude we all have to the regions from which they come, which
is in turn partly judged by the stereotypes that such speakers may
have on radio and television. And many of these stereotypes have
been picked up by radio and television from literature. The fact that
the local people in Hardy's novels speak a south-western dialect has
led many to think of this dialect as quintessentially rural and the
people who speak it as full of homely wisdom and proverbial lore.
Because many people from the South of England never venture to
the North, they tend to think of it as full of factories established in
the Industrial Revolution and of its cities as squalid working-class
areas. Hence those who speak in a northern dialect are often thought
to be hard-working, but poor; honest, but not very well educated.
On the other hand, Cockney speakers may well be regarded as the
archetypal city slicker, as one who will readily fleece visitors to the
capital by exploiting their gullibility. People who come from Scotland may be considered dour and industrious as well as clever.
Since many of the Scots who move South are professional people,
the attitude towards speakers of Scots is quite different from that
towards those from the North of England.

● It needs to be remembered that these are **stereotypes** and bear no
resemblance to reality. You may well know many people who are
regional dialect speakers who are totally different from what you
might anticipate from their stereotype. These stereotypes are socially
motivated, but they are none the less powerful for all that. It requires
an act of will to overcome a prejudice towards a particular speaker

because of his or her pronunciation. Many do not make that act of will, for it is much easier to fit people into general types than to understand each individual. People who exhibit the least amount of localised accent in their speech forms are likely to have lived in several different parts of the country or to have been educated up to university level. Both these experiences bring people into daily contact with speakers of other dialects and thus they may have often modified or lost their original pronunciation.

Since traditionally it is people in professional classes who have moved around the country the most and who have received the highest levels of education, there is an assumption that those whose speech approximates most to Received Pronunciation are likely to be educated and/or professional people. People who have not moved far, if at all, from their original communities will often feel no pressure to change their pronunciation and indeed may have a strong incentive through group solidarity not to do so. Attempts by some have been made to increase the status of local dialects and young men in particular may take a pride in the fact that they speak with a specific dialect. Research has shown that this attitude is much stronger among men than among women, and this is something to which you could well devote a project. Is there a noticeable difference between men and women in your local community in the extent to which they have adapted their speech to Received Pronunciation?

• Naturally what has been written in the previous paragraphs has been seen from the viewpoint of someone from the United Kingdom. Speakers of English who come from other parts of the world, such as Americans or Australians, may not have the same attitude towards regional speech in the United Kingdom, though they may be familiar with some stereotypes such as speakers of Irish or Scots. They are much less likely to distinguish readily between local English dialects just as most people from England would find it difficult to decide whether an American came from the East or the Mid-West. Americans and Australians, for example, have their own differences in language and pronunciation and some of these may be local and some racial. In America there is a sharp difference in the eyes of most speakers between the speech of Blacks and of Whites, and most will detect a difference between the speech of Southerners and Northerners. Some of these differences may be known in England through films and more recently through immigration.

• In the United Kingdom today there are sizable communities of people from the Indian subcontinent and from the West Indies. Many of these people came to England, or their parents did, in the 1960s when there was a shortage of labour and native English people did not want to do many of the menial jobs in society. Some came because they were persecuted in their own countries, such as Uganda, or because they felt they could better themselves by moving to the United Kingdom. As a result of this immigration and the subsequent spread of these communities, white English people have become more familiar with the speech patterns of Indian and West Indian people. 'Indian', of course, is a useful cover term for people from the Indian subcontinent, because most white English people cannot distinguish between the various nationalities (Indian, Pakistani, Bangladeshi or Sri Lankan) or between the various linguistic groups from that area.

Although racial overtones undoubtedly colour the attitudes of some white English people towards the various Indian communities, because Indians are thought to occupy a wider range of occupations than the West Indians, the Indian stereotype is perhaps less derogatory and demeaning than the West Indian one. There are many Indian professional people, particularly doctors, as well as shopkeepers, taxi drivers and those who have more menial occupations. On the other hand, although many West Indian people do fill important and professional jobs, the stereotype is that they occupy the least desirable jobs in society, and many white people assume there is a close link between West Indians and certain specialised cultures such as the drug culture or the Rastifarians. All of these factors colour reactions to the speech of Indians and West Indians. Your own reaction will depend upon your age, social position and your own colour. It would be an interesting project to evaluate how the speech of English people of different racial origins is regarded by others from a similar racial and social mix. You may well find that speech stereotypes differ considerably according to people's racial origins and social position.

• Stereotyping of the English from other parts of the world is less likely here in England because apart possibly from London few places have sufficient concentrations of such speakers to let stereotypes develop. Many English people find it difficult to distinguish an Australian speaker from a New Zealand one and either of these from a South African one. Although many claim to recognise an

American speaker, it is often only the most pronounced accents which they recognise. Individuals may well have their own attitudes to speakers of such varieties as these, but for the most part it is difficult to produce any generalisations about attitudes to the different varieties of English outside the United Kingdom which exists.

Use-related varieties

It is a common misconception that each individual knows only one form of English which he or she uses on every occasion. But we all adjust our language to the **occasion** in which we find ourselves, although as we refer to all the varieties we use as English we may find it difficult to recognise the differences which exist.

• Think of language like dress. We change our clothes to match the social occasion we are going to participate in. If you were going to an interview for an office job, you would probably put on a suit and wear a tie, if you are a male, and put on a suit or outfit with a white blouse, if you are a female. You would almost certainly not put on jeans or wear a track-suit. But if you were going for a job on a building site, you may well decide that a suit was not the appropriate dress for the occasion and you might then put on jeans and an open-necked shirt. If you were going out for the evening to the pub with your friends, you would probably put something casual on, whatever precisely that might be. It is not likely to be a suit. But the clothes you wear will be characteristic of what is worn in the country you live in, though what is worn in your own country is affected by what is worn elsewhere in the world just as your language is affected by words used in other countries.

• It is easier to switch your language from one variety to another than it is to change your clothes and you may do this many times on the same occasion. If you are in a class discussion with a teacher and your fellow students, you may always address your teacher in slightly different terms from the ones which you use to your fellow students. You may even address male fellow students slightly differently from female ones. These changes can be described as **changes in register** or as 'code switching'. We start by considering code switching and then go on to variation in register. Each variety of language you use is a code and you switch to a different code depending on the people you are talking to, the subject matter you are discussing and the environment in which you find yourself.

* The most obvious example is where someone is brought up in an environment of bilingualism or diglossia. Bilingualism is where someone knows two unrelated languages fluently, usually because both have been spoken from a very early age. This situation exists in England among the children of immigrants, particularly those immigrants who have a strong sense of community and want to maintain their culture even though they live in a 'foreign' environment. This applies to many people from the Indian subcontinent, whether they are Muslims or Hindus, and can apply to immigrants from China or Vietnam.

Often a different religion will encourage the survival of a different language and culture. Children of Indian immigrants to England will know a language like Urdu or Hindi, which they will have learned from their families, as well as English, which they will pick up from their friends, the television and school. If the community is tight-knit most social occasions will probably use Urdu, if that is the language of the family, but at school English will be the normal language used. But the situation is not as simple as that. Within the family environment certain subjects may well be conducted in English and English may be used by one parent to the child on more occasions than by the other parent. This itself may depend upon each parent's familiarity with English. If the father goes to work with English-speaking people and the mother stays at home and mixes little with English-speaking people, conversations with the mother will always be in Urdu, but conversations with the father may occasionally switch to English. The children of the family, when they are all of school age, may use English even in the family environment, particularly if they wish to show some kind of peer-group solidarity among themselves against their parents. This is one way in which children could begin to exert their independence. Although situations in which there are monolingual English speakers present will encourage all conversation to be in English, there will be times when the Urdu speakers may wish to say something among themselves which the English speakers should not understand or because in their excitement they fall back on their major language. Equally in the school environment, Urdu speakers may use Urdu among themselves because it is their natural medium of communication in which they exhibit their own solidarity. If you are a bilingual speaker, it would be interesting to keep a diary for a week to record when you spoke one language and when the other, and if possible to decide what were the factors which made you use one rather than the other.

* Diglossia is the situation where there are two separate varieties of a single language, though both varieties are sufficiently different from each other that speakers of the one variety may not readily understand what is said in the other. Often the contrast will be between the standard form of a language and one of the localised varieties. A good example is the German-speaking part of Switzerland, where people know Standard German, which is usually the written and the prestige form, and Swiss German which is the colloquial and familiar form. Similar situations can exist in different parts of the United Kingdom. It could be said that in parts of Scotland two varieties exist, broad Scots dialects and the Scottish form of Standard English. The latter is based on the Standard English in its written form, and as its spoken form is a Scottish adaptation of Received Pronunciation, it is understandable to most English people. Scots, on the other hand, is largely a spoken form, though plays and other written works are produced in it now; it is largely unintelligible to the average speaker of English. The situation in some dialect areas in the North of England comes close to diglossia.

    The same is true of areas abroad where English and an English-based pidgin are both used. A pidgin is a variety of language which is no one's mother tongue. It is used in areas where several languages are spoken as the language of commerce and communication between speakers of different languages in their daily business. Hence an English speaker may well use English to other English speakers, but resort to pidgin when non-English speakers are present.

* Whereas in bilingual situations monolingual speakers will have no idea of what is being said in the other language, in diglossic situations it will be easier for monolingual speakers to have some inkling of what is being said. A German from Germany might well understand some of what was said in Swiss German and would probably not find it too difficult to read what was written in it. Speakers of the two varieties will switch from one to the other according to the situation, though the switching may not

occur in the same environments as in bilingualism. This is partly because with two varieties of a single language there is usually a contrast between a prestige variety and another variety, which carries with it overtones of informality and less status, whereas with two languages each may have status with the speakers. Consequently to switch from English to Urdu may not have the same status implications as switching from English to a dialect, and this will naturally affect when one might switch from one to the other. But there have been attempts to increase the status of these varieties recently and these attempts have met with some success. We will consider some of these questions in relation to Black English Vernacular.

★ Black English Vernacular (BEV) is the name given by the American scholar William Labov to the language of black youths from the ages of 8 to 19 who are members of the young gangs living in inner city areas of big cities in America. It can be said to be a variety of English with its own linguistic system, which has much in common with Black English though it is not identical to it. It also may be said to represent a linguistic stage which these black youngsters pass through, but while it lasts it is one of the most important factors which holds the group together.

• Because the children are black and because their language variety contains many features which have been labelled 'non-standard' in the past, BEV was always considered a corrupt version of English. But BEV stands in the same relationship to Standard English as Swiss German does to Standard German. This is an important relation to bear in mind because speakers of BEV, like speakers of many non-standard varieties in England, were often dismissed as incapable of thought or logical expression because people who knew Standard English thought of their language as not only non-standard, but also sub-standard. Since many educationalists belong to the middle classes and set a premium upon Standard English, the inability of speakers of such varieties as BEV to acquire proficiency in Standard English was regarded as a sign of their lack of intelligence.

This view was given support by the creation of the terms 'elaborated' and 'restricted' codes by Basil Bernstein in 1966, which referred respectively to the languages of middle-class and working-class children in England. Unless working-class children could extend their restricted code to the elaborated code of the middle classes, they would never be able to have access to the learning and other benefits which sprang from knowing that code. It was claimed that the elaborated code uses a more complicated syntax and a Latinate vocabulary, which it was difficult for restricted speakers to acquire. Labov set out to show that speakers of BEV were effective narrators and could think logically and use complicated syntax, provided one understood the variety of English they were using and was prepared to evaluate it without prior prejudices.

• BEV has certain syntactic features which differentiate it from Standard English. The following can be taken as examples. In sentences formed of a subject, part of the verb *to be*, and noun or adjective or present participle in -*ing*, the part of the verb *to be* may be omitted. Thus we find *He a friend*; *He tired*; and *He working tonight*. However, habitual behaviour is usually represented by the invariant form *be* to give *He be always fooling around*, though this can also be represented by the omission of *be*. Where Standard English uses the dummy subject *there* in such sentences as *There is nothing to do*, BEV replaces *there* with *it*.

BEV exhibits **negative concord**, by which all the words in a clause which can have a negative form take it so that one has double or triple negation. Thus one can find expressions like *Down there nobody don't know about no club*. In negative sentences BEV may invert the order of subject and verb which is the way a question is expressed in Standard English, as in *Ain't nobody in my family Negro*. With the lexical verb in the past participle form, the auxiliary is often *been* by itself when it indicates an action which has taken place in the past and is still operative at the time of speaking. Hence the sentence *She been married* means that the woman has been married for some time and is still married; it does not mean that she has been married in the past and is no longer married, which is what speakers of Standard English are tempted to understand it as.

• There are naturally many other features of BEV which it is not possible to go into here. The following is a transcript of a conversation between an interviewer (**In.**) and a fifteen-year old boy (**H**) which has some occasional interventions by the interviewer in brackets. It comes from William Labov's book *Language in the Inner City* (Oxford: Blackwell, 1977), pp. 214–15.

In.: What happens to you after you die? Do you know?

H: Yeah, I know. [What?] After they put you in the ground, your body turns into – ah – bones, an' shit.

In.: What happens to your spirit?

H: Your spirit – soon as you die, your spirit leaves you. [And where does the spirit go?] Well, it all depends . . . [On what?] You know, like some people say if you're good an' shit, your spirit goin' t'heaven . . . 'n' if you bad, your spirit goin' to hell. Well, bullshit! Your spirit goin' to hell anyway, good or bad.

In.: Why?

H: Why? I'll tell you why. 'Cause, you see, doesn' nobody really know that it's a God, y'know, 'cause I mean I have seen black gods, pink gods, white gods, all color gods, and don't nobody know it's really a God. An' when they be sayin' if you good, you goin' t'heaven, tha's bullshit, 'cause you ain't goin' to no heaven, 'cause it ain't no heaven for you to go to.

In this passage many of the syntactic features noted above are to be found and perhaps you can find them for yourselves. This passage also shows that speakers of BEV can relate a position in a coherent way. Once you know the linguistic system you can follow the thought of the piece. Since there are many ideas about god, there cannot be one God. As God is said to have made heaven, there can be no heaven if there is no God. Consequently everyone will go to hell.

LINGUISTIC VARIABLES

Examination of differences within a language used to concentrate on **dialectology**, that is regional differences which were thought to be characteristic of all speakers of a given area. One could thus speak of the dialect of Lancashire as compared with the dialect of Yorkshire. Nowadays more attention is directed at differences which speakers make in their **daily life** as they encounter different social situations. Whereas dialectology in the past often focussed on changes seen from a historical perspective, newer approaches which are often grouped together as sociolinguistics try to describe language in use in a given speech community and to outline how changes are developing within that community.

• Regional dialectologists often based their observations on the speech of one or two old members, particularly males, of the community who had lived there all their lives as though in an attempt to record a dialect before it finally disappeared. Sociolinguistics has gone in the opposite direction by recording the speech of hundreds of people from a speech community, who are selected randomly and drawn from as wide a social range as possible.

It is also important to record the speech of these informants in varying situations. These situations can be conversations which are formal or informal. The first is when an informant answers questions put to him or her by the interviewer, who as a stranger imposes certain constraints on the language of the informant. The second is speech recorded when the informant is talking to friends or family. Equally it is possible to ask an informant to read texts which are graded on a scale of formality to informality. The most formal reading is a list of minimal word pairs, i.e. a pair of words which have a similar pronunciation or which could be confused in some varieties of spoken language such as *fat* and *vat*. The least formal reading could be a passage of prose from a narrative or a newspaper. In this way it is possible to record the language of the informants under differing circumstances to see how their language changes.

• The American linguist mentioned earlier called William Labov also introduced the concept of the **linguistic variable**. Usually a variable in the studies which have been conducted hitherto has been phonological, partly because individual sounds occur so often that it is easy to record their use, and partly because sounds have to be used in all levels of language from the most to the least formal.

Variables can be discrete or not. **Discrete** variables are those which are sounds that are present or absent, and thus are much easier to record. Initial *h-* is a discrete variable, because people pronounce a word like *help* either with initial /**h**/ or without it; there is no intermediate stage. With other sounds it may be the **quality** of the sound which changes and this is much more difficult to record. Thus many Northerners, as we have seen, pronounce words like *grass* with /æ/ rather than with /a/. But those who come in contact with speakers of Received Pronunciation or who feel that the latter sound is a sign of education and status may try to change their /æ/ in the direction of /ɑ/; they will need to alter both the length and the quality of the vowel.

Naturally there are various stages on the road from one sound to the other and it is possible to record the variants used. With a large number of informants it is possible to quantify the various sounds which are produced and to do so by grouping the informants according to age, sex, occupation and social class. To some extent it could be said that the interest is less on the individual and more on the language of the group to which he belongs and how that language differs from the language of other groups or from the language of the same group in different circumstances.

• The results of some enquiries conducted by Labov and others show surprising results. We all use linguistic variables. Even though dropping of initial *h*- is regarded as a marker of low social class by some, we all drop our *h*'s under certain circumstances. Generally speaking the higher in social class and educational attainment we are and the more formal the situation in which we are speaking, the more likely we are to keep initial *h*-. Tables 4.1 and 4.2 (which have been invented) give an impression of the kind of scores one might expect for the retention of initial *h*-.

Table 4.1 Retention of initial *h*- by social class

	Formal %	Informal %
Socioeconomic groups A/B	100	89
Socioeconomic groups D/E	45	10

Table 4.2 Retention of initial *h*- by gender in socioeconomic group A/B:

	Formal %	Informal %
Male	100%	85%
Female	100%	93%

From these tables it can be seen that socioeconomic groups A/B always score higher than socioeconomic groups D/E, but that both change towards *h-* retention the more formal the situation is. Studies have also shown that females are more likely to preserve features of the Standard Language than males even in informal situations. The higher the score, the more the language approximates to the standard. Such studies have shown that it is wrong to claim that higher class speakers always keep their initial *h-* and that lower class speakers always drop it. Sociolinguistic literature is full of tables like those above and they may provide you with ideas as to how you could undertake a small project on similar lines.

• Although much of the work on sociolinguistic variables has been done on the phonological level, it is possible to extend the methodology to embrace other features of language, particularly **morphology** and some points in **syntax**. In BEV the presence of absence of part of the verb *to be* can be defined as a variable. Equally the use of negative concord occurs more often in our speech than some of us like to admit and can also be investigated as a variable. The same might be true of the presence or absence of the ending *-ly* in some adverbs such as *slow/slowly* or of concord between the subject and verb in number. As we saw in the Introduction some people say *'E were* rather than *He was*, though the occurrence of *were* for *was* is likely to be a variable. However, it is not possible to investigate these features at a reading level, because most people will be prompted by what the text in front of them has as to what they say.

VARIATION IN REGISTER

In the newspaper The *Independent* for (20 October 1991) there was a report about the national conference of probation officers at Llandudno. The report began as follow:

> Probation officers wrestled with the problem of neutral language at their annual conference in Llandudno in Wales, which ended yesterday. Speeches at the National Association of Probation Officers were monitored for racism, sexism, disablism, heterosexism, ageism and sizeism. Don Kilbride, from Norwich, presented a report from the monitors and said:

'Language is still a difficulty. "Paymaster" and "turning a blind eye" indicate that we need to remain vigilant.'

● One might comment that it is difficult to think that any language is neutral, because in trying not to offend one group one might offend another. Thus the word *paymaster* was said to be sexist by the monitors because it assumes that the male gender as represented by *-master* is the norm for professional positions of this type. But if one tries to re-write this word as *pay-person* or *payer* or to find another word altogether such as *financial officer*, one might be misunderstood or not understood at all. In English personal pronouns are marked for gender in the third person singular: *he, him* as compared with *she, her*. If one wishes to avoid sexism in language, one will try to avoid something like 'The informant . . . he . . .', if one is referring to the informant as an example of the type of person the researcher has to handle. One might then say 'The informant . . . he or she . . .', and you may have noticed various examples of that type in this book. But it has to be admitted that *he or she* is more clumsy than just *he* and that some people will dislike it because of its clumsiness or even because they object to the way the language is being adapted to avoid sexism. Some people advocate using the plural in these circumstances, though that is not always possible.

● It is considerate to avoid giving offence to others in one's language use, though one has to be very linguistically aware if one is to avoid falling into every possible trap. Many of you probably did not realise that 'to turn a blind eye' could possibly cause offence to the blind, and it is possible that many blind people (or should we say 'visually handicapped'?) might not have noticed this themselves until someone pointed it out to them.

● It is hardly surprising that it is **sexism** which has aroused the most linguistic engineering, because feminism and equal opportunities have attracted great support over the last decades and because English is marked for gender in so many ways. You might argue whether *blind* or *visually handicapped* was the less offensive way of referring to those who cannot see either at all or hardly at all. But the arguments will be about a few words, usually nouns or adjectives, within the language and whether they should be changed. **Gender differences**, as we have seen, permeate far more areas of the language. There are differences in the pronouns, and not only the personal pronouns; in bound and free morphemes such as the suffix *-ess* as in *princess* or the compound element *-man* as in *chairman* or *man-* as in *manmade*; and in a wide range of vocabulary items, including naturally a vast range of titles such as *Lord* and *Lady*. For the most part avoiding offence is a matter of vocabulary and to some extent this is no different from the whole process of using a euphemism such as *passing away* for *dieing*.

But as with all matters concerning words, it is not so much the word itself but **what it stands** for which causes offence and in due course the new word or phrase may come to be considered as offensive as the old one. To replace *old folks* with *senior citizens* is admirable, though there is always the potential danger that *senior citizens* will in its turn come to be regarded as just as pejorative as *old folks*. It is a useful exercise to pick at random a passage from a book or a newspaper and to run through it to see how far it might offend some section of the community because of the connotations of the words used.

• In this matter it is often helpful to consider how other people in the **same community** are referred to. For example, if in a newspaper report about South Africa one came across the expression 'a South African' and 'a black South African', one might reasonably assume that the author was taking white South Africans as the norm so that anyone who was not white had to be specified in some way. In the report from The *Independent* quoted earlier in this section you may notice that it refers to 'Llandudno in Wales', but just to 'Norwich'; it does not have 'Norwich in England'. It might be argued that this report is written from an English point of view for English readers, who need to be informed where Llandudno is, but not where Norwich is. But it is clear that that stance could cause offence to Welsh people wherever they live or to English people living in Wales. It is at best a slightly unfortunate way of putting something in an article which is concerned with neutrality in language.

This example highlights the problem for newspapers about how to present information, what background information may be necessary, and what political problems lie beneath some uses of language. Racial and national issues are particularly important. The year 1991 saw the break-up of the old Soviet empire, as it was sometimes called. Is *empire* a loaded expression, since that country was in name at least a union of Soviet republics? But before 1991 to refer to someone as a *Lithuanian* rather than as a *Soviet citizen* could easily have caused offence to some. Equally those who are native Russians but who live in Lithuania may now have to be called *Lithuanian* – or rather one might have to be clear in a description whether one was referring to the citizenship or race of the person concerned.

• Vocabulary can of course be used in quite the opposite way – to establish **solidarity** among a group of people and to exclude others who are unfamiliar with that vocabulary. To some extent any professional group or any trade establishes its own jargon which helps to create a sense of belonging among those that know the language. Sometimes these can be abbreviations or acronyms and sometimes they can be Latinate and learned words. Certain sub-cultures have developed their own language which can almost amount to a kind of code which keeps others out. The drug culture, the teenage culture, the pop culture all have elements of this, though many of the words used in these three cultures overlap. It is difficult for outsiders to know what some words mean, because they will be ignorant of the connotations which the words possess. Take a word like *heavy*. This word appeared to characterise anything or anyone who tried to impede the spontaneity and classlessness of the teenage culture and so had an unfavourable connotation. But partly through its association with *heavy duty* and *heavy metal*, its connotations have improved over the more recent years, though you may need to move in particular circles to discover what connotations they give to that word.

CONCLUSION

Language is all around us and is an expression of our attitude towards life and other people. It is 'a loaded weapon', as the title of a book on language by Dwight Bolinger claims. We reveal ourselves through the language we use, and in this chapter we have tried to give you some understanding of how this is so and how you may both realise and investigate some of the differences. It is hardly surprising that sociolinguistics or the relation of language to society should have become such an important subject over the last fifty years. But it is such a vast subject that we have been able to do little more than give you some inkling of the interaction between language and society. It is an area in which many exciting and worthwhile projects could be undertaken.

EXERCISES AND ESSAY QUESTIONS

1   Take cuttings from several newspapers about some domestic event and compare to what extent they differ in their use of language which could be described as sexist.

2   Take cuttings from several newspapers preferably of different political persuasion and readership about some foreign event, such as for example in the new Commonwealth of Independent States (formerly the Soviet Union) or in South Africa, and examine how far the reports remain neutral in respect of racial or possibly racial language.

3   Tape a conversation at home between as many members of your family as possible and then examine it to see whether the language contains examples of racism, sexism, disablism, heterosexism, ageism or sizeism.

4   From the same tape monitor how much each person speaks and whether their contribution can be evaluated in terms of status or gender. To what extent do some participants try to exclude others from the conversation by interrupting them or by not letting them have their turn in the conversation?

5   Conduct a test on yourself by reading lists of minimal pairs, of single words and of a continuous piece of narration. Evaluate how your own language changes according to what you are doing.

6   What is meant by a 'standard language' and how many people in England use it?

7   Explain how you would recognise a Scots speaker, a West Country speaker and a Cockney speaker and describe what your reactions to each of these speakers is.

8   Make a list of words you use which your parents do not and try to explain when you use them and what they mean.

9   Think of as many different words as you might use to express the concepts *good*, *bad*, *beautiful* and *ugly*, and explain when you might use each one.

5

Applying Language Study to Texts

INTRODUCTION

In earlier chapters we have discussed broad categories of English which we have identified according to historical, social or geographical criteria. Within these categories, however, it is possible to identify further differences which may cross these boundaries or be contained within them. These differences, and the uses to which they are put, are what we mean by **style**. The chief factors which govern the choice of style are the purpose for which the language is being used and the relationship between the users and the field of discourse – the 'use-related variants' referred to in Chapter 4. As native speakers of English we may recognise and use many of these differences instinctively, but it is important for us, as language students, to be able to identify the linguistic features which characterise different styles of discourse, to discriminate between their effects, and to assess their effectiveness.

• Language can be transmitted and perceived as **speech** or **writing**, and it is usual when discussing varieties of style to distinguish between these two media.

★ Speech can be transcribed and writing can be read aloud, but there are marked linguistic differences between the two forms which we should note.

★ Besides words, spoken language also uses non-verbal features to communicate meaning. These include gesture, facial expression, eye-contact and the proximity of the speaker to the listener.

★ Spoken English uses stress and intonation patterns, loudness and accent; in written English these have to be replaced by an

elaborate system of punctuation, though this is less eloquent than
the resources of spoken English.

* Speech is spontaneous and feedback is instantaneous. Consequently, the structure and meaning of a spoken utterance can be
changed while it is in progress. It can be repeated, rephrased,
further explained, or even left unsaid as the speaker reacts to the
audience's response. This accounts for 'the features of normal
non-fluency' – pauses, hesitations, repetitions and self-correc-
tions – which we always find in speech. As there is no immediate
feedback from written English, the writer must tailor his
language very carefully to fit the content, the context, his own
point of view and the audience he is addressing.

* There are some grammatical differences between speech and
writing. Speech uses contracted forms, *aren't, they're, I've,* and
tag questions, *aren't you?, haven't they?, didn't I?*. These are much
less common in written English and their use reduces the
formality of the discourse. Lexical choice also contributes to this
effect and generally speaking, speech is less formal than writing.

• But there are many stylistic features which spoken and written
texts **share**. Although in this chapter we deal with various forms of
written language only, we hope that many of our observations will
be seen to be applicable to spoken varieties.

• It is not unusual for a single text to contain a variety of
heterogeneous stylistic features, such as a lexical item from an
unrelated field of discourse as a metaphor, or a grammatical form
which is more usually associated with a different purpose. But
before looking in detail at some longer passages, we should
perhaps consider what stylistic features we might expect from
specific texts.

STYLE ACCORDING TO PURPOSE

A popular A level English Language syllabus requires candidates to
submit examples of writing for different purposes and nominates
entertainment, persuasion, information and instruction as possible
types. Although not exhaustive, these four broad categories cover
most of the day-to-day linguistic purposes we have to deal with as
either users or recipients of the written word.

To inform

Writing to inform probably elicits the most straightforward language of the four types. Consider the following piece of information:

1   The school will close for the Christmas holidays on 20 December, and will reopen on 6 January.

An announcement of this sort is likely to be found posted on a school noticeboard or in a letter sent home to parents. The audience, although clearly defined, is wide ranging, both in terms of age and of social and educational background. In spite of this, the message is clear to all. The vocabulary is simple; words are used denotatively, with literal meanings. Structurally, the sentence is a compound one, with two simple clauses joined by 'and'. There is nothing unusual about the order in which the clause elements are arranged; in each clause the verb is preceded by the subject and followed by the adverbial(s), giving the structure **SVAA** for the first clause, and **(S) VA** for the second, as the subject, being the same as that for the first clause, is not repeated.

The complexity of informative language is likely to increase as the audience becomes more specific and the field of discourse becomes more specialised. This can be shown by the following passage:

2   As TGAT said: 'Assessment in the secondary phase must take account of emerging subject emphases at 11, and reflect a very largely subject based organisation in the pre-14 stage and later up to 16 when it must articulate with GCSE and Records of Achievement (ROA).' There may therefore be less scope for a pupil's knowledge and use of English to be assessed through other subjects. (*National Curriculum, English for Ages 5 to 16* 14.21 (London: Department of Education and Science, 1989).)

• This document was written to provide information about the proposals for a National Curriculum in English. Although the document was intended to reach a wide audience of people with an interest in educational matters, the primary target was teachers and others who are professionally engaged in education.

• This audience is most clearly identified by the lexis which is used. *GCSE* is an abbreviation which is widely understood, but *TGAT* will be understood only by those who have read the document in full, as it is explained in a footnote to paragraph 1.5. *Records of Achievement* is an expression with a specialised educational meaning, and we must understand that 11, 14 and 16 in this context refer to the ages of pupils. Words such as *secondary*, *subject* and *pupil* all have a variety of meanings, but their use together here shows clearly that the context is one of education.

• The paragraph consists of two sentences. An analysis of their structure shows the first to be a complex sentence which also shows some compounding of clauses, and the second to be a simple sentence. In both sentences the order of clause elements is usual and unambiguous. Any apparent difficulty in understanding these sentences arises from the length of some of the elements of structure, especially subjects and objects. The noun phrases which comprise these structures contain much information, mostly by means of a high degree of postmodification.

• The writers know that they are addressing an educated audience who are used to reading and comprehending prose of some complexity. They do not wish to seem much cleverer than their audience, nor to patronise them by using too simple a style. The choice of lexis and grammatical structures is in itself a signal from writer to reader. By showing that they 'speak their language', the writers attempt to create a bond between themselves and the audience.

To instruct

Instructional writing also requires straightforward language, and as with information, the more general the audience, the less specialised the language will be.

3   Take one tablet three times a day after meals.

This is the familiar instruction we have all seen on the label of a medicine bottle. The audience for this text could not be more general, since anyone is likely to fall sick, yet the instruction is precise. The vocabulary is unambiguous. The text consists of one sentence which has the structure **VOAA**. There is no subject because the verb is in the imperative form. It is, moreover, a transitive verb.

The regular use of the imperative form of transitive verbs is a characteristic of instructional writing and provides the formulaic nature of many of the commonest and most frequently encountered sets of instructions, such as how to polish your shoes:

4   Apply polish with a soft brush;

or how to work a vending machine:

5   Insert 10p . . .

Transitive verbs can also be used in their passive form:

6   One tablet *to be taken* three times a day.
7   The eggs *are beaten* separately then added to the dry ingredients.

Passive verb phrases which contain a modal verb are frequently found in instructions:

8   After opening, the contents *should be stored* in the refrigerator.
9   The wire which is coloured blue *must be* connected to the terminal which is marked with the letter N or coloured black.

The same range of verb phrase structures can be found in instructions for quite specialised procedures:

10a Undo and remove the bolts and spring washers securing the engine steady arm bracket and right-hand lifting bracket to the cylinder head.
10b Undo and remove the bolts and spring washers securing the radiator bracket and left-hand lifting bracket to the cylinder head.
10c The six shaped bolts which hold the camshaft cover to the top of the cylinder head should now be unscrewed in a progressive diagonal manner. Lift away the cover and the gasket.
10d The crankshaft should now be turned until the timing marks ¼ tdc on the flywheel are in alignment with the

pointer, and number 1 cylinder on commencement of the firing stroke.
(J.M.Haynes and B.L. Chalmers-Hunt, *Austin Allegro Owners Workshop Manual*, p.19 (Sparkford: Haynes 1988).

- Most of us would have no difficulty in recognising this as part of a set of instructions taken from a car repair manual. The publishers of the manual tell us that 'the tasks are described and photographed in a step-by-step sequence so that even a novice can do the work'. This defines the audience; in theory, anyone who can read; in practice, those who are mechanically literate or wish to be so.

- Any difficulty we might experience in understanding the text arises from the **technical vocabulary**, in particular the nouns, and especially those with multiple premodification, such as *engine steady arm bracket*. In the manual, these words are explained by reference to diagrams. The steps in the procedure are arranged in a logical order, in short paragraphs which are labelled as a further help to the reader. The complexity is in the noun phrases, where both pre-modification and postmodification are used uniquely to identify the engine components.

- **10a** and **10b** are parallel in structure. Each consists of a compound sentence with the structure **V** and **VO**. Both verb phrases are the imperative forms of transitive verbs, and the object is shared by the two verbs. **10c** contains two sentences. The second is a simple sentence with an imperative verb phrase. The first sentence in **10c** and the sentence in **10d** contain passive verb phrases, 'should . . . be unscrewed' and 'should . . . be turned'. The modal verb *should* which is included in these verb phrases expresses obligation and, like the modal verb, *must*, is often found in instructional writing when the writer needs to emphasise a point. Its use also has the effect of reinforcing the writer's authority. The sentences in **10c** and **10d** also contain adverbials. The single word adverbial *now* follows the modal verb in each, but the longer adverbials which particular-ise the actions immediately follow the lexical verbs, giving the order **SVA** within the sentence. The straightforward ordering of clause elements coupled with the precise denotation of nouns is what makes the instructions comprehensible and easy to follow.

Field-specific lexis and imperative and passive verb phrases are characteristic of instructional writing though, as we shall see later, these features can be affected by other factors in the text.

To persuade and to entertain

The two other categories, persuade and entertain, are alike in that they do not necessarily use language in a straightforward way. Rather than simply conveying the message the language is frequently foregrounded, standing between the message and the reader, drawing attention to itself. In times past, from Ancient Greece to the Renaissance, such use of language was taught as rhetoric. Devised by the ancients as a means of persuasion for use in the law courts, it gradually became the stock-in-trade of the poets, a way to divert and delight. Modern writers, on the whole, no longer study the theory, but they still imitate the practice. This is perhaps most evident in their use of figurative language and the careful ordering of the units of language in ways that create patterns.

• The most commonly used figures of speech include **metaphor**, **personification** and **puns**. A metaphor is a figure in which one thing is described in terms of another thing from which it is quite different except for one shared attribute.

11   Throughout the negotiations the Chairman was an old fox.

A fox's most widely recognised attribute is his slyness or his cunning, so referring to the Chairman as a fox highlights his deviousness. In a metaphor the comparison is implicit. When the comparison is explicit, using *like* or *as*, it is called a **simile**:

12   The old man was as sly as a fox.

Personification is a figure in which an object or an idea is given animate characteristics.

13   The wind whispered in the trees.

By using a verb which signifies a sound made by a human voice, the wind becomes a character rather than a meteorological phenomenon. Similarly, in

14   The thunder growled in the distance

the use of this particular verb imbues the thunder with the characteristics of an unfriendly and possibly dangerous animal.

The following passage from William Golding's *Lord of the Flies* shows how figurative language can be used to good effect.

15   Smoke was rising here and there among the creepers that festooned the dead or dying trees. As they watched, a flash of fire appeared at the root of one wisp, and then the smoke thickened. Small flames stirred at the bole of a tree and crawled away through the leaves and brushwood, dividing and increasing. One patch touched a tree trunk and scrambled up like a bright squirrel. The smoke increased, sifted, rolled onwards. The squirrel leapt on the wings of the wind and clung to another standing tree, eating downwards. Beneath the dark canopy of leaves and smoke the fire laid hold on the forest and began to gnaw. Acres of black and yellow smoke rolled steadily towards the sea. At the sight of the flames and the irresistible course of the fire, the boys broke into shrill, excited cheering. The flames, as if they were a kind of wild life, crept as a jaguar creeps on its belly towards a line of birch-like saplings that fledged an out-crop of the pink rock. They flapped at the first of the trees, and the branches grew a brief foliage of fire. The heart of the flame leapt nimbly across the gap between the trees and then went swinging and flaring along the whole row of them. Beneath the capering boys a quarter of a mile square of forest was savage with smoke and flame.

(William Golding, *Lord of the Flies* (London: Faber, 1954) pp. 48–9)

Throughout the description the fire is compared with a series of animals which increase in size and power as the fire grows stronger. The comparison is sometimes explicit: *like a bright squirrel, as if they were a kind of wild life, as a jaguar creeps*. The smallest animal is suggested by *crawled*, and the largest by *swinging and flaring*. In fact, much of the work in this description is done by the verbs. *Crawled, scrambled, leapt, laid hold, began to gnaw* are all dynamic verbs which we would expect to have animate subjects. Metaphor, simile and personification are used to sustain the comparison through several sentences, though they are not, of course, the only features which create the effectiveness of this description.

• **Puns** are wordplays which exploit language's inherent ambiguity. Though many people profess contempt for puns, they have always been popular with writers especially in the past. Nowadays, puns are frequent features of advertising language and newspaper headlines, for example, the words FACE VALUE were used to introduce an advertisement for cut-price cosmetics, and the headline 'Identity Photos still on the Cards' appeared above a story in the *Guardian* newspaper about the possibility of putting photographs on credit cards. In both these examples the pun is a device for attracting attention; in the first one because *face value* is not what we expect an advertisement to offer, and in the second because we would not normally expect the non-standard expression *on the cards* to be used so prominently in a quality newspaper.

• Advertising often draws on a variety of media, which may include pictures and sounds, but in the advertisement for the Peugeot 205 GTi (see Figure 5.1) the message is carried entirely by the language.

★ The headline is eye-catching, in large letters taking up about three-quarters of the page. It seems to be making an offer to older car users, *anyone between 50 and 70*. Unusually for an advertisement the name of the product is not very prominent, and this helps to sustain the deception which is continued in the left-hand column of the text below the headline. In fact, not until the third paragraph of this text do we realise that it is a car's performance and not that of an elderly person that is being discussed, that *between 50 and 70* refers to miles per hour, not years of age.

★ The first three sentences of text copy the lexis and style of an advertisement for a patent medicine. Rhetorical questions suggest to the consumer some symptoms which he probably does not have though the vagueness of these symptoms does give them a universal application. This vagueness is matched by a coyness which is typical of the semantic field of patent medicines. *A lack of vitality* and *a certain sluggishness* are euphemistic expressions for describing illness. *A good tonic, clinical tests* and *fast-acting* also belong to this semantic field though *clinical tests* also represents an appeal to authority. By this stage, of course, we are aware that the product is a car.

★ The right-hand column of the text mingles technical data, the sort of field-specific lexis you would expect to find in a car advertisement, with more typically patent medicine advertising language. *That extra boost of energy just when you need it* and

Figure 5.1

The perfect car for anyone between 50 and 70

As you approach the half-century, do you suffer from a lack of vitality?

Do you experience a certain sluggishness and find you can't get around as quickly as you'd like?

If so, you are clearly in need of a good tonic. We recommend the 205 GTI.

Clinical tests show it to be remarkably fast-acting for people from 50 to 70 (6.6 seconds in fourth, to be precise.)

A Bosch L-Jetronic fuel-injection engine provides that extra boost of energy just when you need it.

Its low centre of gravity and low-profile tyres give increased sharpness and mobility.

And all-round independent suspension maintains your equilibrium even when the pace is at its most hectic.

The 205 GTI. Take it every day to help you get up and go.

ACCELERATION FIGURE FROM CAR MAGAZINE. FOR MORE INFORMATION ON THE PEUGEOT RANGE FREEPHONE 0800 678 800.

references to *sharpness, equilibrium* and *the pace* create the bright and cheery tone that is also a cliché of such advertisements. The final exhortation to *take it everyday to help you get up and go* sustains the tone to the end.

The effectiveness of this advertisement depends for the most part on the ambiguity of the language, but linking the car so closely to the idea of a patent medicine also produces a most effective metaphor. The message is that this car is not only a good car, it also makes you feel better.

• **Verbal** and **syntactic patterning** is also a way of drawing attention to the ideas which are being discussed. Language patterns can be achieved in several ways; these include simple repetition, repetition of a word or a phrase at the beginning or end of successive sentences, and the repetition of syntactic structures. The last of these is all the more striking when it includes an element of variability within the structure. By substituting a word of similar meaning or a word of opposite meaning for a word already used, an idea can be explained, enlarged or presented more forcefully. Language patterns are familiar from their use in proverbial expressions; for example.

16 One man's meat is another man's poison.
17 Spare the rod and spoil the child.

In each of these proverbs the wisdom is encapsulated in two expressions which are **syntactically parallel**. The first contains two noun phrases separated by *is*. The headwords of the noun phrases, *meat* (here with its older meaning of 'food'), and *poison*, are opposite in meaning; the expressions are linked by the shared premodifier *man's*, and further distinguished by the opposition of *one* and *another*. The second proverb consists of two parallel clauses linked by *and*, each clause containing a transitive verb in its base form whose object is a noun phrase consisting of a headword and the determiner *the*. The verbs are further linked by the alliteration of /**sp**/. Patterns are also frequently found in liturgical language, helping to make it more memorable. We all recognise the words of the marriage service:

18 . . . to have and to hold from this day forward, for better for worse, for richer for poorer, in sickness and in health, to love and to cherish, till death us do part.

In this we can notice the two parallel synonymous infinitives, *to have* and *to hold* which are balanced by a similar pair, *to love* and *to cherish*. Each of these pairs has an adverbial of time, in the form of a prepositional phrase, which takes account of all possible available time. The middle of the expression consists of six prepositional phrases arranged in pairs; the antonyms (words of opposite meaning) which comprise the prepositional complement in each pair constitute a series of inclusive formulae which, linked to the time adverbials, cover the vicissitudes of married life and leave nothing to chance.

• Language patterning is often used to good effect in **persuasive writing**. Consider the following extract from 1992 election material published by the Labour Party:

19   A nation where vibrant, growing industry produces world
     class products and brands. A country which can afford the
     best in health care and education for its citizens. A country
     proud to take its place in a free and democratic Europe.
     The contrast between our vision and the Tories' policies of
     muddle and restraint could not be greater. We want to
     take Britain forward into the next century. They want to
     take us back into the nineteenth century, back to private
     health care, back to private education, back to private
     railways and water companies and mines.
     (The Labour Party, *An Election Letter* (London, 1992).)

★ The first paragraph consists of three minor sentences which describe Labour's vision of a modern, prosperous Britain. The first foresees thriving industry, the second flourishing health and education services, the third membership of an improved Europe. The three separate ideas are presented as three separate linguistic units with no overt structural link between them. However, the ordering of these units implies that the content which is being expressed represents a series of logical developments, and this idea is reinforced by syntactic patterning. Each minor sentence consists of a noun phrase in which there is complex postmodification but no premodification. This has the effect of highlighting the headwords of the noun phrases; *nation* in the first is varied by its near-synonym *country* in the second, and *country* is repeated in the third. It is this repetition which links the units together. The similarities of the postmodification by relative clauses in the first and second and by a reduced relative clause in the third is also part of the pattern, as is the repeated use of co-ordinate structures, *products and brands, health care and education, free and democratic.*

★ In the second paragraph, the *contrast* of the subject of the first sentence is emphasised by antithesis and syntactic parallelism in the second and third sentences. These two sentences are linked by having the same verb, but the subjects *we* and *they* are opposed. The adverbials *forward* and *into the next century* in the second sentence are opposed by *back* and *in to the nineteenth century* in the third. The implications of this backward step are then plainly stated in three syntactically parallel structures which repeat *back* but vary in prepositional phrases to highlight the election issues. A further link between these phrases is the repetition of *private*. A list with three elements is a notable feature of rhetorical patterning. We find it here in the three adverbials, and also in the three co-ordinate nouns with which the paragraph ends. Throughout these two paragraphs, lexis and structure are yoked together to convey the information in a way which is designed to move the reader.

APPROACHING TEXT ANALYSIS

The task of applying language study to texts is basically the same whether the text we are considering is a short unseen passage in an examination or part of a longer project, a literary text or a non-literary text.

• The **stylistic** features which are important will vary according to the text and the kind of text we are dealing with, that is, a text may have certain features which are characteristic of the **genre** to which it belongs, such as newspaper style or advertising style, but there will also be features that are peculiar to each text. 'Style' includes features of language and features of presentation. Under presentation we need to consider such formal features as layout – is a text set out as a poem, a letter, a list, a recipe, a 'wanted' poster, or any other standardised format which can affect the communicative potential of a text? We also need to consider the typography of the piece, including the use of capital letters, italics and possibly even such non-linguistic features as logos and trade marks.

• The overall **structure** of a text is important, as is the way in which the content is **organised**: the order in which it is presented and whether it takes the form of or includes narrative or dialogue.

• **Language** features will include spellings and the sounds they represent, vocabulary and meanings, grammatical structures and figurative language. The sorts of questions we need to ask about any text are: Is it written in Standard English? If not, in what ways does it differ from Standard English? Does the lexis include any dialectal words, slang or colloquial terms, or terms from a particular register such as business or religion?

It can be useful to consider the **classes** of word which are used. For example, does a text contain a lot of adjectives or adverbs, or have nouns and verbs been chosen for their descriptive force? Are nouns concrete or abstract? Do noun phrases contain a lot of information, and if so, is this because of premodification or postmodification? Are verbs stative or dynamic, active or passive, are modal verbs a feature of this text? Pronouns may be important. Is the text narrated in the first person or the third person, and does the writer address the reader directly? The length and structure of sentences can also be a useful guide to assessing a writer's intentions. If figurative language is used, its type and frequency need to be taken into account. Alliteration, rhyme and onomatopoeia are connected with sound, but they can be used to good effect even in a text which is intended for silent reading, while irony and metaphor can be indirect ways of expressing a point of view.

• We consider all these features, but our final analysis will be a discussion of only those which are **relevant**. A stylistic analysis is not a list of the stylistic features of a text; it is a discussion of those features which produce a **specific effect**. Nor should it be confused with literary criticism. We do not need to discuss the content of a description, agree or disagree with an argument, or pass a judgement on a character. We do not ignore these matters, but our primary concern is the way language is used in their expression.

Often, a brief reference to the content is a good way into a stylistic analysis, but there are no hard and fast rules for how such an analysis should be undertaken. With some texts, a line of approach is suggested even before they are read; with others, a single reading will reveal some salient points, but there will always be some texts which will not yield up their secrets without a struggle. With non-literary texts consideration of **purpose** and **intended audience** may provide a good lead, but if the audience is very general and there is more than one strand to the purpose, the usefulness of this approach may be limited. In these cases, the questions suggested above should prove fruitful. At all events, we must never lose sight of the fact that it is the language of texts we are studying, and any comments we make should be dependent on and supported by reference to specific linguistic features.

Recipes

As examples of this methodology in practice, we will now look at some analyses of texts. They are offered to give you some idea of how some kinds of texts might be tackled and not as comprehensive treatments of the texts. We would encourage you to enlarge or modify our analyses, or to make your own, perhaps approaching the texts from a different angle.

Text A

Gazpacho

8 large ripe tomatoes
2 cloves garlic
1 cucumber
½ onion
1 green pepper
6 × 15 ml spoons (6 tablespoons) olive oil
lemon juice to taste
1 × 400 ml (14 fl oz) can tomato juice
salt and pepper
ice cubes

Chop the tomatoes roughly and peel the garlic. Place in a liquidizer and liquidize thoroughly. Skin and dice the cucumber. Peel and roughly chop the onion. De-seed and dice the pepper and add to the liquidizer. Liquidize again. Season well and rub the puree through a large sieve or vegetable mill. Chill well.

Just before serving, put the soup back in the liquidizer and add the oil gradually, liquidizing all the time. Add lemon juice to taste, and some ice. Mix in the tomato juice (previously chilled).

Note This soup is best served very cold. Small bowls of skinned, de-seeded and chopped tomatoes and cucumber, diced blanched pepper and croutons of fried bread can be served as accompaniments, but this may not be very convenient on a picnic. As an alternative, sprinkle freshly chopped herbs over the soup, after pouring it into serving bowls.
(*Cooking for Special Occasions, by Mrs Cozens* (London, Macdonald Educational in association with WI Books Ltd, 1979), pp. 40–1).

Text B

Chilled Spanish gazpacho
(serves 6 people)

This is a truly beautiful soup for serving ice-cold during the summer and it's particularly refreshing when the weather is hot. However, please don't attempt to make it in the winter as the flavourless imported salad vegetables will not do it justice.

1½ lb firm ripe tomatoes (700 g)
One 4 inch piece of cucumber, peeled and chopped (10 cm)
2 or 3 spring onions, peeled and chopped
Half a large red or green pepper, seeded and chopped
2 cloves of garlic, crushed
4 tablespoons olive oil
1½ tablespoons wine vinegar
1 heaped teaspoon fresh chopped basil, marjoram or thyme (depending on what's available)
About ½ pint cold water (275 ml)
Salt and freshly milled black pepper

For the garnish:
Half a large red or green pepper, seeded and very finely chopped
One 4 inch piece of cucumber, peeled and finely chopped (10cm)
2 spring onions, finely chopped
1 hard-boiled egg, finely chopped
1 heaped tablespoon fresh chopped parsley
Salt and freshly milled black pepper
4 ice cubes

Begin by placing the tomatoes in a bowl and pouring boiling water over them; after a minute or two the skins will loosen and slip off very easily. Halve the tomatoes, scoop out and discard the seeds and roughly chop the flesh.

Now place the tomatoes, cucumber, spring onions, crushed garlic and chopped pepper in a liquidiser, adding a seasoning of salt and pepper, the herbs, oil and wine vinegar. Then blend everything at top speed until the soup is absolutely smooth. (If your liquidiser is very small combine all the ingredients first then blend in two or three batches.) Taste to check the seasoning and pour the soup into a bowl. Stir in a little cold water to thin it slightly – anything from ¼ – ½ pint (150 – 275 ml) then cover the bowl with foil and chill thoroughly.

To make the garnish, simply combine all the ingredients together with a seasoning of salt and freshly milled black pepper, and hand them round at the table together with small croutons of bread fried till crisp in olive oil, well drained and cooled.

Serve the soup with four ice cubes floating in it.

(Delia Smith, *Delia Smith's Cookery Course Part Two* (London, BBC Publications, 1979), pp. 312–13.)

• Of all instructional writing, the cookery recipe is probably the most formulaic. It is usually in two sections, 'ingredients' and 'method'. The ingredients section is most often set out as a list of what is required to make the dish. Each item in the list is a noun phrase and the noun is frequently premodified, for example, *8 large ripe tomatoes* in text A. However, if the noun phrase contains a quantifier, we may find that determiners are omitted, for example, *½ onion*, rather than *½ 'an' onion*. Similarly, when the quantity stipulated is itself a noun phrase, as in *1 . . . can*, and the ingredient is expressed as a postmodifying prepositional phrase, the preposition *'of'* is often omitted, for example, *1 . . . can tomato juice*. This is what we find in Text A. The 'method' section most often consists of a series of sentences which are either simple or compound and which contain imperative verb phrases. These verbs are mostly transitive. When the object is the same as in the previous clause it is usually omitted, and is not even referred to by use of a pronoun, for example, *De-seed and dice the pepper and add to the liquidiser*. The 'method' section of Text A is also conventional. The lexis is all drawn from the semantic field of cooking, and some words and expressions, such as *dice, to taste* and *blanched* are quite specialised. The instructions are given in a carefully arranged logical order. A little extra infomation is given in the section headed '**Note**'. The lexis of this section is very conventional, but there is some attempt to vary the sentence structure. Two declarative sentences are followed by an imperative sentence, though this is varied by having an adverbial as the first element. Also, the non-finite clause which is the final element of the sentence denotes an action which in real time precedes that of the main verb.

• The entire recipe is presented very formally. The writer makes no attempt to strike up a relationship with the reader. We do not learn anything about Mrs Cozens, except that she is clearly a very competent cook.

• Text B is very different. It more or less follows the conventional recipe layout with a list of ingredients followed by a method, and uses reduced prepositional phrases following expressions of quantity. However, the author's personality is stamped on this recipe from the very beginning. She is anxious to promote her recipe in the introductory paragraph using the adjectival phrases *truly beautiful* and *ice-cold*. Contracted forms such as *it's* and *don't* reduce the formality of the text and help to modulate the very authoritative tone in which her strong opinion is expressed in the second sentence. Many of the sentences in the method section follow the conventional pattern of the imperative of a transitive verb followed by the object, for example, *Halve the tomatoes*, though the object of her verbs is nearly always stated. An example of how she varies her clause structure is found in the first sentence of the method section, where present participial clauses are used to denote the sequence of actions following the main verb *Begin*. The use of *Begin* to start the method linked with the adverbial *Now* at the beginning of the third sentence and *Then* at the beginning of the fourth has the effect of demystifying the procedure, an effect which is heightened by *slip* in line 2 and *simply* in line 14. *Top speed* refers to the fastest setting of the liquidiser, but as this collocation is frequently found with the meaning *very fast* and with a suggestion of ease, it also helps to promote the idea that the recipe is easy. *Floating* in the last sentence helps to create an image of the finished product.

The differences in these two texts reflect the different audiences they were written for. The Women's Institute book, Text A, is written for the experienced cook who understands the technical terms and knows that *Gazpacho* should be made only in summer. The would-be cook is committed to the task and the writer has no need to intervene. Delia Smith, on the other hand, has produced a cookery *Course*. Her readers may be novices who do not know some of the basic facts, such as how to blanch tomatoes. Alternatively, it may just be that they are not committed. At all events, Delia Smith mediates between the reader and the recipe, persuading them to cook as well as teaching them how. Her advice, opinions and enthusiams are made more acceptable by the friendly tone in which they are couched, and her friendliness itself made more acceptable because we recognise her from our television screens, and can link the words with a voice and a face. Each text, in format, lexis and grammatical structures is designed to suit its audience.

Newspapers

Newpapers have a complex function in our culture. They not only **inform** us about what is happening in the world, they also **filter** the news so that the version of a story we receive depends on our choice of newspaper. Newspapers can be classified in different ways, but a primary distinction is between the broadsheets and the tabloids. These two categories are often referred to as 'quality' and 'popular' respectively, since the tabloids have a much wider circulation than the broadsheets which give a more 'in-depth' coverage of events and contain, it is alleged, fewer trivial stories than the tabloids. Important and interesting matters are usually reported by both sorts of newspaper and a comparison of the same story in the two different types of newspaper makes an interesting exercise. A typical approach would be simply to consider the similarities and differences between these two versions of the same story (shown in Figures 5.2 and 5.3), published on 30 January 1989 in the *Mirror* and *The Independent* newspapers respectively.

● *The Two Stories*

⋆ Both passages deal with the same basic fact, that a German businessman is thinking of setting up a kidney dealing business

Figure 5.2

Kidney dealer rumpus

A GERMAN count wants to set up a kidneys-for-sale base in Britain.

Already he earns £5.000 for every organ deal he arranges abroad.

And he expects to sell nearly 100 kidneys in the next year at prices of up to £30,000.

But last night the National Kidney Research Fund condemned his plans saying they could wreck the present kidney donor system.

Moral

Businessman Rainer Rene Count Adelmann van Adlemannsfelden, speaking in Birmingham, said he felt no guilt about the organ deals.

"It is hard work because the moral thinking is against me," said the 41-year-old father of ten.

But NKRF director general James Wellbelove warned that the count's scheme must not be allowed happen in Britain – and may be needed to prevent it.

(a)   Tabloid version

• *The tabloid story*

Headline: Kidney dealer rumpus.

Structure: This consists of a noun phrase in which the headword *rumpus* is premodified by another noun phrase, *kidney dealer*. The use of a noun phrase as a premodifier is typically tabloid style.

Lexis: *Rumpus*, meaning 'row' or 'trouble', belongs to a less formal register. *Kidney* and *dealer* are, when taken singly, ordinary unmarked words with straightforward denotative meanings. As a collocation, however, the phrase has a sinister meaning since it implies trading in human organs. That a row has developed concerning this trade is suggested by the headline, but this does not suggest any editorial bias.

125

(b) Broadsheet version

'Kidneys for sale' business may open

A GERMAN businessman is set to open a "kidneys for sale" operation in Britain, matching donors willing to sell the organs with people waiting to buy them.

Rainer Graf Adelmann, who already acts as middleman in the organ trade in West Germany, believes opening the market will alleviate the suffering of both the healthy poor and the sick rich.

The Department of Health last night condemned his plan but admitted it was powerless to stop it. "The department would be totally opposed. We would have to consider what further action to take," a spokeswoman said. But she added that there was no law prohibiting payment for organs.

Mr Adelmann first announced his plan on Central Television during a discussion programme on the controversy surrounding recent allegations that a number of Turkish peasants received payment for kidneys used in transplants operations at the Wellington Humana Hospital, a private clinic in St John's Wood, north London.

Mr Adelmann intends to set up a contact point in Britain for people wanting kidney transplants. He says he has 800 potential donors in West Germany and can arrange for the operations to be done in Paris, Austria or the Far East.

He earns £5,000 for every organ deal he arranges and expects to sell nearly 100 kidneys in the next year. "I have no problem in getting kidneys. I charge 20 per cent for myself for my work, but it is easy money," A donor can receive up to £30,000 for a kidney.

- *The broadsheet story*

Headline: 'Kidneys for sale' business may open.

Structure: This consists of a complete sentence. The verb phrase *may open* has a modal verb which shows that there is still some doubt whether the events with which the story is concerned will ever come about. The subject of the sentence is a noun phrase in which the head word *business* is premodified by another noun phrase *'kidneys for sale'*. As well as being a typical newspaper style construction, *'x for sale'* is a formulaic expression. Again it is the collocation of *kidneys* and *for sale* which catches the attention of the reader and provides the frisson which makes him read on. There is no apparent editorial bias in the headline but the use of the word *business* and the possibility that such a business may open, suggest that in a materialistic economy all businesses may be equally valid.

in England. Both papers report that the business is already in operation on the Continent, and mention the price each donor can expect to receive and the businessman's commission. The broadsheet gives more background detail about what the business entails and what has led to the present episode.

* The tabloid story is written in seven paragraphs in a single column with a secondary headline between paragraphs 4 and 5. Each paragraph contains one sentence, though paragraphs 3 and 4 each begin with co-ordinating conjunctions, and technically paragraphs 2, 3, and 4 are a superordinate clause. This kind of layout and sentence structure is typical of tabloid newspapers. It is easier to grasp the meaning at first reading, and the tabloids aim at a wide readership covering a broad spectrum of reading ability.

* The broadsheet story, though longer, has only six paragraphs arranged in four columns under a long horizontal headline. This arrangement allows for a longer headline which can be more explicit than the single-column headline that the tabloid layout allows. Two of the paragraphs (3 and 6) contain direct speech and consist of several sentences, and paragraph 5 also contains two sentences. This story is written in complete sentences which contain both co-ordination and subordination. The sentences are quite long, and the length is achieved mostly by postmodification in the noun phrases. This is particularly the case in paragraphs 1 and 4 which provide the background information, and in paragraph 2 which provides information about the businessman.

* **Noun phrases** also contain much information in the tabloid story, but here the nouns are premodified: *Kidneys for sale base*; *the present kidney donor system*; *NKRF director general James Wellbelove*. Premodification rather than postmodification of nouns produces the shorter punchier sentences which are typical of tabloid style, and which add to the impression that this is straight-to-the-point hard-hitting journalism. However, such premodification is also used in the noun phrase *the 41-year-old father of ten*, where the information conveyed is of no relevance to the subject matter. Such irrelevancies are also clichés of tabloid style.

* The **lexis** of the stories is similar in that they both draw on the semantic field associated with organ transplantation, and as befits its (alleged) readership, the broadsheet is slightly more technical than the tabloid, though it is less technical than an article on the same paper's 'Health' page would be.

★ There is a difference between the **tone** of the two stories. The broadsheet story is apparently unbiased, and the first paragraph makes the German neither more nor less blameworthy than the patients he wishes to deal with. *Matching* is a technical word, but its use here has the effect of matching donors and recipients in morality as well as tissue type. This idea is continued in the second paragraph, in the antithesis and syntactic parallelism of *the healthy poor and the sick rich*, though there is here perhaps a hint of irony based on the implication of 'amoral' as part of the sense of *sick*. This idea reinforces the implied criticism of the headline. There is, however, no explicit editorial disapproval. Opposition to the plan is expressed in a direct quotation by a Department of Health spokeswoman, but even she is not entirely forthright in her condemnation, using the modal verb *would* which picks up the *may* of the headline to imply that the sale of kidneys is still only a possibility.

★ Explicit criticism in the tabloid story is conveyed in a reported comment from the Director of the National Kidney Research Fund whose views on the matter are very definite. However, by referring to the German businessman as a *Count* and giving him his full title the paper stresses his aristocratic origins and may be making a political point. The broadsheet does not mention the Count's background. Also, it refers to Mr Adelmann's intention as a *plan*, a neutral word, while in the tabloid it is a *scheme*, a word with connotations of underhand dealings. The subsidiary heading *Moral* certainly raises the question of the morality of the enterprise, and the use of the word *guilt* even though it is in a negative form, suggests to us what our reaction should be.

★ Both stories leave us feeling that the sale of human organs is wrong. The tabloid's story is rather more emotional than the broadsheet's and gives us slightly less information in rather simpler language. The tabloid's doubts are expressed in the vocabulary while the broadsheet's are in the grammar, but in each case the story is written in a way that will strike a chord with the paper's readership.

Radio

The following text was broadcast on Radio 4 just before 9 o'clock on a Sunday morning. Although this is a spoken text, it is not spontaneous speech; so it does not show any of the normal features of spoken language. It is, in fact, written language being read aloud. Let us identify those features of the text which are likely to effect the desired response in the audience.

Appeal on behalf of the Mental Health Foundation by Professor Anthony Clare (BBC Radio 4, 3 February 1991.)

As children, we gazed up at the night sky and had our first disturbing encounter with infinity. As adults, we came to understand the vast distances involved, the staggering changes out there, and how very much more was left to discover. We accepted the idea of the universe as the last frontier; certainly it is the last frontier beyond the planet Earth. Down here, though, down to earth, we have a matching last frontier: the challenge of mental health. I'll use no cold statistics here because big numbers all too easily distract us from the intense, personal, human suffering of mental illness. Few adults in Britain are not touched by it directly or indirectly. For one out of every ten of us it snatches away any chance of a balanced, satisfying life and relentlessly sucks in our relatives, friends, neighbours, colleagues. That's what we fear about mental illness. No wonder we see it as some kind of black hole.

The good news is that there's much more light on the subject than that. In the mental health universe there are bright stars everywhere: charities specialising in particular mental illnesses and handicaps; charities and groups run by superbly committed people – doctors, nurses, volunteers who work in the here and now to tackle the effects; who make life bearable now for the sufferers, and make it workable now for the carers.

But coping now is not enough. We want to know why Alzheimer's disease can so cruelly steal from you your mother's awareness or ability to communicate, and whether this mental illness might one day happen to you. We want to know why your child was born autistic and has somehow become lost in an outer space all his own, and how this mental handicap can be diminished for the living, and avoided one day for the as yet unborn. Take, for example, someone I know, John, aged eighteen, a boy making the transition to adulthood. He is disintegrating from the ravages of schizophrenia. We can manage his condition, but we're desperate to have more light shed on the complex inner turmoil he must endure. We need more light, too, on all the varieties of stress and depression that can develop into breakdown, addiction, suicide or crime.

And that's where the Mental Health Foundation comes in. We need urgent cash support to keep up vital grants to medical scientists undertaking voyages of discovery for us. We need cash, too, for grants to fund projects searching out new ways of dealing with mental illness in the community. Great break-throughs await us. All that holds us back is lack of money. We ask your backing for the scores of eminent medical and social action professionals of the mental health field who give their time free to navigate this exploration for us. They make the cash-granting decisions for the Mental Health Foundation, and there's a queue of potential breakthrough projects before them marking time for lack of funds, all ideas that may be lost without your help because the Foundation relies absolutely on voluntary income. There could be nothing more crucial you could do with your £10 or your £10,000. Your gift, when translated into urgent research action, really can help save someone you love from becoming lost in space. One day, indeed, it might even save you. As a psychiatrist I know first hand just how much research can do for us. So can you make a credit card donation? The number to call is 081 992 5522. That is, 081 992 5522. The lines will be open until eleven o'clock this morning, or you can send a cheque or postal order made out to the Mental Health Foundation Appeal to me, Professor Anthony Clare, MHF, PO Box No.7, London W3 6XJ. (That is, PO Box No.7, London W3 6XJ.)

On behalf of the Mental Health Foundation, I thank you.

• This appeal by Professor Anthony Clare on behalf of the Mental Health Foundation is aimed at an adult, rather middle-class, fairly well-off, thinking audience. We can infer this because of the time of the broadcast, 8.50, Sunday morning, Radio 4, when listeners would be perhaps preparing to go to church; the economic status of the audience is suggested by *credit card, cheque book* and the minimum donation mentioned; the age of the audience is suggested in paragraph 3: they are old enough to be parents, and to have parents old enough to be suffering the ill effects of age.

• The appeal is persuasive at several **levels**. Professor Anthony Clare is a well known and respected figure from the world of mental health, and this makes the appeal authoritative. By the use of the first person plural pronoun in the first paragraph he flatters the audience by identifying with them in their understanding of space. This use of the pronoun also helps to create the tone of the appeal which is, on the whole, quite friendly. He uses abbreviations such as *I'll, that's*; colloquial expressions such as *the good news is* help to maintain this tone. However, *We* in the third and fourth paragraphs refers to Professor Clare and his fellow carers in the mental health field. His easy shift from member of the the public to professional carer takes the audience with him and causes them to identify with those who care.

• The **content** of the appeal is in itself persuasive. Mental illness is unpleasant, widespread and still not fully understood; there are many people who willingly alleviate its effects; the need for research is being met but needs funds.

★ Professor Clare begins by appealing to the **minds** of his audience. His reference to a *balanced, satisfying life* suggests that this is what his audience enjoy; it is an oblique appeal to their self-interest as it can be destroyed by mental illness. He presents his material in a way that will appeal to their understanding. In the first paragraph he introduces the metaphor of the universe to explain what mental illness is like. In the first two sentences this metaphor works on three levels: children do not understand as much as adults, so as adults we now have a greater appreciation of what space and mental illness mean; children can be taken to mean former ages, when mental illness was little understood; and as the human race has progressed our understanding of mental illness has developed. *Children* can also mean the mentally ill, people living in innocence and ignorance whom it is our duty as more fortunate *adults* to look after. This metaphor is continued and developed effectively throughout the appeal, from *the last frontier* of paragraph 1, through the idea of light in paragraph 2, and the *outer space* of autism and the need for light in paragraph 3 to the *voyages of discovery* in the final paragraph. Throughout the appeal the lexical field of astronomy is closely linked with the technical terms associated with mental illness: handicaps, Alzheimer's, autistic, schizophrenia, stress, depression, breakdown. None of these terms is explained in any detail; their use further defines the audience and reinforces Dr Clare's relationship with them.

★ Despite the overt appeal to the minds of the audience, the heart is not ignored; Professor Clare uses some very stirring language. He uses abstract nouns to refer to mental illness but it is personified by the use of verbs such as *snatches away, sucks in* and *steal*; and even some of the abstract nouns such as *ravages* and *turmoil* imply a violent and unpleasant activity. The persuasion is aided by the use of many rhetorical devices, such as the parallel beginnings of the first two sentences reinforced by the antithesis of *children* and *adults*. The repetition of *last frontier* on which the metaphor hinges, and of *now* in paragraph 2 which emphasises the valuable work the charities are doing at present and links up with the hopes for the future expressed in paragraph 3. Several lists are used for emphasis: *relatives, friends, neighbours, colleagues; breakdown, addiction, suicide or crime*. The syntactic parallelism of *make life bearable now for the sufferers* and *make it workable now for the carers* suggests the close relationship between all concerned with mental health. *I'll use no cold statistics here*, declares Dr Clare before going on to give us the most important statistic. Such a denial of what you intend to do is a well-known rhetorical device designed to gain the audience's sympathy. In this case *cold* is offset by *intense, personal* and *human*, the premodifiers of *suffering*.

• The way in which the material is **structured** is persuasive. The first paragraph gives us some unpleasant but non-specific information about mental illness; the second expresses optimism in a non-specific way. The third paragraph returns to the facts of mental illnes, and is not only specific but personal. Specific diseases are mentioned, but it is not any old woman who is suffering from Alzheimer's disease, it is *your mother*. This emotional reference to the closest of human relationships is maintained in the reference to *your [autistic] child*. The example of *John* is very specific, but *disintegrating, ravages, complex inner turmoil* are not clinical medical terms, but words designed to stir our emotions. The final paragraph returns to optimism and is specific. By contributing to this appeal the audience can help to alleviate this suffering. Again repetition is used for emphasis; *urgent* and *breakthroughs* both occur twice, as does *cash* which is varied by synonyms *money, grants, funds, income*. Once an actual amount has been mentioned this becomes *your gift* in which the cash is closely connected with the donor. The return to the space metaphor reiterates the points made in paragraph 3, while *One day,* *indeed, it might even save you* is a direct appeal to human selfishness. Dr Clare's reference to himself underlines his authority in these matters.

• The appeal is persuasive in all these ways, and the time limit of two hours on credit card donations is designed to give a final boost to the audience's good intentions.

Literary texts: prose

Although all writers use language in a self-conscious and deliberate way, this is particularly true of the writer of a literary text which is designed to be more permanent than the other texts we have considered so far. The effects, which may seem effortless, have not been achieved by chance: they have been designed, and the end of analysis is to find the design.

> But the rain came for three days, with only half a day to follow it of low cloud and soaked air; so that housewives hung what linen there was to wash before smouldering fires that dirtied more linen than they dried; and then there was wind and rain for a week. When he came out of his deanery, cloaked for the hurried passage to the cathedral, he would see the clouds at roof level so that even the battlements of the roof were blurred by them. As for the whole building itself, the bible in stone, it sank from glorification to homiletics. It was slimy with water streaming down over moss and lichen and flaking stones. When the rain drizzled, then time was a drizzle, slow and to be endured. When the rain lashed down, then the thousand gargoyles – and now men thought how their models mouldered in the graveyards of the Close or the parish churches – gave vent. They uttered water as if this were yet another penalty of damnation; and what they uttered joined with what streamed down glass and lead and moulding, down members and pinnacles, down faces and squared headlands to run bubbling and clucking in the gutter at the foot of the wall. When the wind came, it did not clear the sky, but cuffed the air this way and that, a bucketful of water with every cuff, so that even a dean must stagger, pushed from behind; or leaning against a gust like a blow, find his cloak whipped out like wings. When the wind fell, the clouds fell too and he could no

longer see the top half of the building; and because of the drizzle he lost the sense of the size of it. Therefore the approaching eye had to deal with a nearer thing, some corner of wet stone, huge in detail and full of imperfections, like a skin seen too close. The reentrants on the north side – but there was no direction of light to show which was north and which south – stank with the memories of urination. The flood waters by the river, spread over the causeway, took no account of the guards at the city gate, but invaded the greasy streets. Men and women and children crouched by what fire they had and the smoke from damp logs or peat formed a haze under every roof. Only the alehouses prospered.

(William Golding, *The Spire*, pp. 51–2) (London: Faber, 1964).

This is a descriptive passage which centres around a cathedral and its Dean. The author's main purpose here seems to be to create a mood of depression which he does by stressing the negative significance and connotations of the lexis.

• The key sentence in this description is: 'As for the whole building itself, the bible in stone, it sank from glorification to homiletics.' The cathedral, which should be an expression of God's greatness and glory, has been reduced to an instrument of chastisement to man; instead of stretching upwards to reach God, the cathedral is trapped on earth, surrounded by squalor and decay. This is evoked through the vocabulary, through references to dirty washing, foul-smelling corners, greasy pavements, flaking stone and men mouldering in graveyards.

• As this is a physical description we might expect to find a great many **concrete nouns**, and so we do. Most of these concrete nouns are from two semantic fields: architecture and meteorology. The many architectural features which are mentioned (battlements, roof, pinnacle, etc.), contrast with the single abstraction *glorification* and help to show the cathedral as an earthly rather than a spiritual entity.

• Among the meteorological words *rain*, *water*, and *wind* are prominent, and are given an unpleasant signification. Water, the source of purity and a life-promoting force, is here only a negative force. It prevents the fires from burning, dirties the washing and makes the building slimy. When water comes into contact with man the result is not purification, but urine, which pollutes the exterior of the building. The weather is shown to be a punishment to man, and this is achieved by the collocation of meteorological words such as *rain, drizzle, wind* and *water* with words connected with mental and physical punishment: *to be endured, lashed, penalty, damnation, cuffed, a blow* and *whipped*. So far from being a life-force, water is at last seen as the enemy, as *invaded* suggests, while *flood* brings connotations of destruction. The cloud which obscures the sky and the loftier parts of the cathedral is the cloud of unknowing which obscures God from man, and distracts man's mind and concentrates it on imperfections. The wind, shaping the Dean's cloak into wings, shows him as a fallen angel, trapped in this squalor and ignorance, instead of where he should be, as God's representative on earth.

• Throughout the passage the work of description is largely done by the verbs. Dynamic verbs, frequently connected with punishment, give a sense of movement and sound: *lashed, uttered, to run bubbling and clucking, cuffed, pushed, whipped*. As many of these verbs have inanimate subjects, the use of such verbs has the force of metaphor. The repetition of *drizzled . . . drizzle* emphasises the dismal nature of what is being described. The final sentence, *Only the alehouses prospered*, seems like a positive statement, but the connotations of *alehouses*, drunkenness and debauchery, suggest that in this atmosphere only sin can flourish.

The passage is an example of the 'pathetic fallacy' in which inclement weather is linked with a religious character and setting in order to establish a mood of malevolence and foreboding.

Literary texts: poetry

It is often a good idea to start analysis of a poem by summarising its **content**. The content is not the same as the **meaning**, which may not be apparent at a first reading. A careful appraisal of the poet's language is usually the best pathway to discovering what he has to say. Also, if a poem has a recognisable form we need to consider why the poet chose to use it, and whether it makes any contribution to our understanding of the poem.

Going, Going

I thought it would last my time
The sense that, beyond the town,
There would always be fields and farms,   3
Where the village louts could climb
Such trees as were not cut down;
I knew there'd be false alarms   6

In the papers about old streets
And split-level shopping, but some
Have always been left so far;   9
And when the old part retreats
As the bleak high-risers come
We can always escape in the car.   12

Things are tougher than we are, just
As earth will always respond
However we mess it about;   15
Chuck filth in the sea, if you must:
The tides will be clean beyond.
– But what do I feel now? Doubt?   18

Or age, simply? The crowd
Is young in the M1 cafe;
Their kids are screaming for more –   21
More houses, more parking allowed,
More caravan sites, more pay.
On the Business Page, a score   24

Of spectacled grins approve
Some takeover bid that entails
Five per cent profit (and ten   27
Per cent more in the estuaries): move
Your works to the unspoilt dales
(Grey area grants)! And when   30

Your try to get near the sea
In summer . . .
It seems, just now,
To be happening so very fast;   33

Despite all the land left free
For the first time I feel somehow
That it isn't going to last,   36

That before I snuff it, the whole
Boiling will be bricked in
Except for the tourist parts –   39
First slum of Europe: a role
It won't be so hard to win,
With a cast of crooks and tarts.   42

And that will be England gone,
The shadows, the meadows, the lanes,
The guildhalls, the carved choirs.   45
There'll be books; it will linger on
In galleries; but all that remains
For us will be concrete and tyres.   48

Most things are never meant.
This won't be, most likely: but greeds
And garbage are too thick-strewn   51
To be swept up now, or invent
Excuses that make them all needs.
I just think it will happen, soon.   54

(Philip Larkin, 'Going, Going', 1973, from Philip
Larkin in *Collected Poems* (London: Marvell Press
and Faber & Faber, 1988).)

In this poem by Philip Larkin the overt subject matter is some of the
changes which have occurred in England in the second half of the
twentieth century, which the poet seems to perceive as changes for
the worse; in particular he is disturbed by the rate at which the
changes are proceeding.

• The poem is written in **stanzas of six lines**, each of which rhyme
abcabc. These stanzas are used to shape the content. The first deals
with changes in the countryside (fields, farms, trees); the second
with changes in the towns (streets, shopping, high-risers); and the
third with the natural environment (earth and sea). The fourth

stanza lists the consequences of the increase in population, the fifth refers to the pursuit of affluence and the sixth is a comment on the speed of change. The last three stanzas draw these ideas together and look ahead to future developments.

• The **external structure** which the verse form provides is, however, a rather loose one, and there are two reasons for this. The first is that there is no regular metrical pattern. This makes the poem's rhythm much more like the rhythm of ordinary speech, an impression which is reinforced by the way syntactic units run over not only from line to line, but also from stanza to stanza – a technique known as **enjambement**. The second is that ideas often start in the preceding stanza. Stanzas 1 and 2 comprise a single sentence; stanzas 3 and 4 are linked by the three rhetorical questions which span the boundary between them. From stanzas 3 to 6 the switches and swerves of the poet's thought appear to grow out of the words he uses: *doubt* is opposed to *age* which in turn suggests *young*; the *more* which the kids are screaming for in the cafe provokes the idea of other needs or wants they will have; their demand for increased pay leads to thoughts on the economy; estuaries remind him of the sea. Most of stanza 6 and the whole of stanza 7 comprise a single sentence, with the last line of stanza 6 and the first three lines of stanza 7 being parallel clauses with the same grammatical function. Stanzas 7 and 8 express the same idea, but while 7 dwells on the negative aspects which will remain, 8 lists the positive aspects which will be lost.

• Although he is addressing a serious subject, the poet does not always use serious language! His language is very accessible in so far as there are no hard words and most of the words he uses have only one syllable. The resemblance to speech which we have already mentioned is heightened by the use of a lot of colloquial language. In addition to contractions such as *there'd* and *isn't* we find words and expressions such as *false alarms, mess it about, high-risers, if you must, kids* and others, such as *chuck* and *snuff it* which are downright slang. This banal language matches the bleakness of his vision of the new landscape and is part of the means by which he conveys his point of view. Although he uses the adjective *bleak* in line 11, he prefers to let nouns with negative connotations carry the burden of description. Thus we have *louts, high-risers, filth, slum, crooks and tarts, concrete and tyres, greeds and garbage.*

But some more 'poetic' language is also used in support of his argument. Amongst this figurative language we notice personification in the use of the verbs *retreats* and *come* in stanza 2 to express the struggle between the past and the present, and the list of noun phrases beginning with *more* in stanza 4 emphasises the inevitable consequences of more people. The collocation of *spectacled* with *grins* in stanza 5 conjures up a sinister image of the business world. This is continued in the pun on *per cent* by which the poet suggests that the true cost is twice the businessman's profit, and the ironic command to *move/Your works to the unspoilt dales* where *unspoilt dales* are also ironically equated with *Grey areas*.

• The ideas expressed in this stanza provide a possible explanation for the poet's dislike of the changes: they are all the result of a desire for material profit. This idea is continued in line 42, where *crooks and tarts* suggest that England is prostituting its heritage for financial gain, and that those who profit from it do so illegally. Throughout the poem alliteration is used to good effect. /k/ and /t/ link the *crooks and tarts* who are spoiling the country with the *concrete and tyres* which will remain, and these two compound noun phrases are further linked and highlighted by being the last words in succeeding stanzas. The alliterative *fields and farms* at the beginning of the poem is balanced by the *greeds/And garbage* with which it ends; the /gr/ of *greeds* echoing the *Grey area grants* and sinister *grins* of stanza 5.

• The idea of change is also expressed by the **verbs** which change from past tense at the beginning of the poem through present tense in stanzas 4, 5 and 6 to a mixture of present and future in stanzas 7–9. This is accompanied by a movement from possibility to certainty in the change from the modals *would* and *could* in the first stanza to the dominant *will* in the last three.

• The poem also contains a high proportion of **adverbials**, and two-thirds of these are adverbials of **time**. They range from single words such as the repeated *always* and *now* to subordinate clauses: *when the old part retreats; before I snuff it*. This suggests a preoccupation with time, which combines with the questions at ll. 18–19

> – But what do I feel now? Doubt?
> Or age, simply?

to provide another possible strand of meaning, in which the poet is lamenting the passing not just of old England but of his own youth, for which the changes become a metaphor, the rate of change a reflection of how time appears to speed up as we get older, and the reference to his own death in line 37 a memento mori.

Idiomatic expression combined with figurative language in a recognisable poetic form is the means by which Larkin makes this comment on the twentieth century, which links environmental changes to materialism and his own passage from youth to age. The poem's title, 'Going, Going', supports this interpretation, suggesting both progressive movement, a journey, and the language of an auction in which England is being sold to the highest bidder.

EXERCISES

Here are additional texts which you may like to analyse yourself or which could be used as a basis for discussion in class. Two are literary texts (**3** and **5**) and the others are non-literary. **1** is from a quality newspaper (the *Independent*); **2** is an advertisement which appeared in a young persons' music magazine; **4** is the foreword to a book about the problems of mathematics; and **6** is an advertisement which appeared in the colour supplements of most newspapers in 1992. Whatever the text, you should always look for the effects produced by the lexis and meanings, grammatical features, structure, figurative language and other linguistic ways in which the writer tries to influence the reader's response.

1 *The Sacked Preacher* (The Independent, *10 February 1992*)

Sacked preacher to reclaim citadel of the Lord

By David Nicholson-Lord

IT MIGHT have gone down well in Ulster, but the islanders didn't like it. If this is evangelism, they said, then give us the quiet life.

The Rev Tom Winter, 60, is not exactly your ton-up vicar. But the changes he introduced at Newport Congregational Church an the Isle of Wight proved too much for the elder brethren. Out went the traditional prayer books and the organ. In came a young Christian praise band, modish contemporary prayers and a style regarded by the staider members of his flock as excessively dynamic.

New blood filled the pews, but older blood boiled with indignation. Bad blood resulted. Mr Winter was accused of neglecting the elderly and being interested only in youth.

Church members convened a special meeting at which they voted 18–12 to sack him. They changed the locks, hired other preachers.

Last week the final blow came. A special sub-committee of the Congregational Federation said it could not change the decision. Nor would he be recommended for another ministry.

But Mr Winter was born in Northern Ireland. He is heir to the great traditions of Paisleyism. The spirit of "no surrender" asserted itself.

Later this month he will attempt to retake the citadel of the Lord in the company of two of his former worshippers, whom he has labelled "minders". He will return to lead services and preach again in his church. One of his minders is a prison officer, the other has a black belt in judo.

Mr Winter says the vote to get rid of him failed to reach the necessary 75 per cent majority. He says he has been "inundated" by calls to come back.

"Congregations have dwindled from over 100 to around 17 since I have been away. I hope I am not heckled or disrupted and if I am I will remind people they are in the house of God. But if that fails my two minders will ask any troublemakers to leave and escort them out if necessary. I do not expect any trouble, but I have been too trusting and naïve of certain people in the past and I am not going to take any chances this time."

The Newport church deacons declined to comment.

2 RAP 1

Yo! Casio present the freshest keyboard ever, Rapman. With 30 RAP patterns and a special "scratch" disk, it's one to make your massive green with envy.

Auto Rhythms kick in 30 different beats, so you can make the freshest sounds around.

Make yourself heard with the mini microphone and change the breaks with the voice effecter in full effect. Rapman runs off the mains or you can take it to the street with the on-board batteries.

Check out Rapman for yourself at your local Casio dealer and hear just how safe you can sound for just £69.99.

3   'As soon as I got to Borstal' (from The Loneliness of the Long
    Distance Runner, by Alan Sillitoe, pp. 7–9)

As soon as I got to Borstal they made me a long-distance cross-
country runner. I suppose they thought I was just the build for it
because I was long and skinny for my age (and still am) and in any
case I didn't mind it much, to tell you the truth, because running had
aways been made much of in our family, especially running away
from the police. I've always been a good runner, quick and with a big
stride as well, the only trouble being that no matter how fast I run,
and I did a very fair lick even though I do say so myself, it didn't
stop me getting caught by the cops after the bakery job.

You might think it a bit rare, having long-distance cross-country
runners in Borstal, thinking that the first thing a long-distance cross-
country runner would do when they set him loose at them fields and
woods would be to run as far away from the place as he could get on
a bellyfull of Borstal slum-gullion – but you're wrong, and I'll tell
you why. The first thing is that them bastards over us aren't as daft
as they most of the time look, and for another thing I'm not so daft as
I would look if I tried to make a break for it on my long-distance
running, because to abscond and then get caught is nothing but a
mug's game, and I'm not falling for it. Cunning is what counts in this
life, and even that you've got to use it in the slyest way you can: I'm
telling you straight: they're cunning, and I'm cunning. If only 'them'
and 'us' had the same ideas we'd get on like a house on fire, but they
don't see eye to eye with us and we don't see eye to eye with them,
so that's how it stands and how it will always stand. The one fact is
that all of us are cunning, and because of this there's no love lost
between us. So the thing is that they know I won't try to get away
from them: they sit there like spiders in that crumbly manor house,
perched like jumped-up jackdaws on the roof, watching out over the
drives and fields like German generals from the tops of tanks. And
even when I jog-trot on behind a wood and they can't see me
anymore they know my sweeping-brush head will bob along that
hedge-top in an hour's time and that I'll report to the bloke on the
gate. Because when on a raw and frosty morning I get up at five-
o'clock and stand shivering my belly off on the stone floor and all the
rest still have another hour to snooze before the bells go, I slink
downstairs through all the corridors to the big outside door with a
permit running-card in my fist, I feel like the first and last man on the
world, both at once, if you can believe what I'm trying to say. I feel

like the first man because I've hardly got a stitch on and am sent against the frozen fields in a shimmy and shorts – even the first poor bastard dropped on the earth in midwinter knew how to make a suit of leaves, or how to skin a pterodactyl for a topcoat. But there I am, frozen stiff, with nothing to get me warm except a couple of hours' long-distance running before breakfast, not even a slice of bread-and-sheepdip. They're training me up fine for the big sports day when all the pig-faced snotty-nosed dukes and ladies – who can't add two and two together and would mess themselves like loonies it they didn't have slavies to beck-and-call – come and make speeches to us about sports being just the thing to get us leading an honest life and keep our itching finger-ends off them shop locks and safe handles and hairgrips to open gas meters. They give us a bit of blue ribbon and a cup for a prize after we've shagged ourselves out running or jumping, like race horses, only we don't get so well looked-after as race horses, that's the only thing.

4
J.J. Sylvester 'Foreword' from I. Stewart, The Problems of
Mathematics *(Oxford: Oxford University Press, 1987)*

Foreword

Mathematics is not a book confined within a cover and bound
between brazen clasps, whose contents it needs only patience
to ransack; it is not a mine, whose treasures may take long to
reduce into possession, but which fill only a limited number of
veins and lodes; it is not soil, whose fertility can be exhausted
by the yield of excessive harvests; it is not a continent or an
ocean, whose area can be mapped out and its contour defined:
it is as limitless as that space which is too narrow for its
aspirations; its possibilities are as infinite as the worlds which
are forever crowding in and multiplying upon the astronomer's
gaze; it is as incapable of being restricted within assigned
boundaries or being reduced to definitions of permanent
validity, as the consciousness of life, which seems to slumber
in each monad, in every atom of matter, in each leaf and bud
cell, and is forever ready to burst forth into new forms of
vegetable and animal existence.

JAMES JOSEPH SYLVESTER

5 '*On Wenlock Edge*', *from the* Collected Poems of A.E. Housman (*London: Jonathan Cape, 1939*)

XXXI

On Wenlock Edge the wood's in trouble;
His forest fleece the Wrekin heaves;
The gale, it plies the saplings double,
And thick on Severn snow the leaves.

'Twould blow like this through holt and hanger
When Uricon the city stood:
'Tis the old wind in the old anger,
But then it threshed another wood.

Then 'twas before my time, the Roman
At yonder heaving hill would stare:
The blood that warms an English yeoman,
The thoughts that hurt him, they were there.

There, like the wind through woods in riot,
Through him the gale of life blew high;
The tree of man was never quiet:
Then 'twas the Roman, now 'tis I.

The gale, it plies the saplings double,
It blows so hard, 'twill soon be gone:
To-day the Roman and his trouble
Are ashes under Uricon.

6   '*How to talk to your cat*', from **Your Talking Cat** (*Colchester: Carnell Ltd, 1992*)

HOW TO TALK TO YOUR CAT

Your cat is talking to you. Listen! – your cat is telling you how much she loves you. Watch! – the special friend who shares your life has so much to say to you about his feelings and needs...if only you know how to listen and what to look for.

If you're a cat lover like me, and wish to better communicate with your pet for a deeper, more loving relationship, then you'll want to find out **HOW TO TALK TO YOUR CAT.** Remember – there's a lot more cat talk than 'Meow'. In fact . . .

There are nineteen different ways cats say 'meow'. And each has its own special meaning! Cats also talk in body language – with their ears, whiskers, eyes and tail... with their poses and movements! **YOUR TALKING CAT** shows you **how to talk to your cat**, how to interpret your cat's meows, facial expressions and often intricate body language, and answers at last fascinating mysteries of feline behavior such as:

• Why your cat rubs you to show affection

. . . and how best to show her yours.

• Why your cat circles in your lap before settling down.
• Why your cat always seems to come over when you're reading or doing paperwork . . . and the ultimate toy to distract him.
• Why your cat doesn't like to be stared at.
• What kinds of toys and games your cat likes best.

And there is also a 'Cat Talk' Chart translating your cat's language, so you'll know when your pet is happiest . . . and illustrated charts of feline facial expressions and tail positions that reveal the range of your cat's moods and feelings.

You may be surprised to discover the warmth and strength of the bonds of affection between you and your cat once you understand her unique language of communication . . . when you learn the secret of **HOW TO TALK TO YOUR CAT.** Order your copy of **YOUR TALKING CAT** today – now, using the handy coupon below:

To: Carnell Ltd., Brook Barn, Main Road, Alresford nr. Colchester, Essex CO7 8AP.

Please rush me my copy of **YOUR TALKING CAT – How to talk to your cat** – at £9·95 (postpaid) on the understanding that if not delighted I can return it within 30 days for a full refund.

☐ I enclose my cheque for £9·95 (Payable to Carnell Ltd)

☐ Please charge my credit card:

Account No. _____ (Visa/Access)

Name _____ BLOCK

Address _____ CAPITALS

_____ Postcode _____ PLEASE

Signed _____ Date _____

Please allow up to 21 days for delivery. We hope to be able to make a variety of further interesting offers from reputable companies – if you prefer not to receive such offers, please write to Carnell Ltd. at the above address.
INM/05/10

6

Undertaking a
Language Project

TAKING STOCK

Before embarking on a language project, you should take stock, which means establishing what is available to you and what your interests are.

Equipment

The first, and perhaps simplest, matter is equipment.

• Do you own a **tape recorder**? If not, can you borrow one? It is no good thinking of a project which involves recording spoken language unless you have access to a tape recorder, and to undertake such a project you will need more or less exclusive use of it.

Access to a recorder is not in itself sufficient. You have to know of what **quality** it is. You may have a recorder which is good enough for recording music played loudly, but it may not be very good for picking up conversation in a noisy environment where several people are speaking, often at the same time. A poor recorder might pick up someone near the microphone, but not others who are some way away.

Equally important, how **adep**t are you at recording? You can clearly pick up some of the techniques as you go along, but this takes time and money. So you might care to consider whether you have a teacher, who both can and would provide some instruction in the technique of recording conversation. Tape recorders are like all machines: you need to have the machine **available** whenever you want to use it, it needs to be **reliable** so that it does not break down, and you need to be able to use it effectively.

• Another item of equipment is a **personal computer** or **word processor**. Do you have one of your own or, if not, can you get access to one fairly easily either at college or at one of your friends' houses? What programmes are available to you? For many projects it will be sufficient to have some easy-to-use software. But if you plan to collect a lot of data it will be helpful to have some computing facility which will enable you to call up the data in particular forms and categories.

Equally important is the matter of how used you are to using a personal computer and what additional help would be available to you as and when you require it. Here we should perhaps add a word of caution about this type of equipment. You should always take **back-up copies** of your work so that you do not lose your data through some error. It is necessary to show how you have worked to produce the final project. This means taking **print-outs** of the intermediate stages of your project as well as of your data. Although this material will not necessarily form part of the finished project, it may be needed to show that the work is your own, to check your results and to explain how you arrived at the final version.

Support

The second aspect includes the support you have available.

• Some topics that you might want to pursue for your project could involve you in some reading and this naturally raises the question of **library** support. Check what is available in your own institution's library and in your local authority library. If you live in a city or big town, the local library is likely to be better provided. If you live near a university or other institution of higher education, you may be able to make use of their library. If you are a member of such an institution, you will naturally be able to use its facilities.

Support also includes the expert, moral and financial help you can get. Your teachers may inform you that your planned project is not something they are expert in and that they may not be able to offer you as much guidance as you could need. This does not mean you cannot do the project, but it may make you think twice about it. It is possible that if you live near a university or polytechnic, particularly one with an English Language Department, you will be able to get help from one of the lecturers there.

Are your parents supportive of and sympathetic to the work you are doing? If so, are they prepared to spend time and perhaps money in helping you either by buying books or equipment for you or by finding out where you can get access to what you need? If you are a mature student, is there a question of available time if you are responsible for your family?

Availability of data

A third aspect is availability of data.

• Let us look at an example. You may be interested in the question of language acquisition and decide that you will compare a child's language over a six-month period. Clearly this is not possible unless you have **access to a young child**. There are not many people of seventeen or eighteen who have brothers or sisters of about three. If you are already a parent you may have a child of that age.

Even if you have access to a child, you may be wise to reflect on some of the **problems** that could arise. You have to make sure that the parents will not accuse you of interfering in the child's language development if its progress is not as fast as the parents think it should be. There is also the **time factor**. To take some sample recordings six months after you made the initial recordings could mean that you are left with insufficient time to evaluate the data you have accumulated.

If you are going to do a project which involves recording speech you need to make sure that people will **agree to co-operate** with you. You will probably find that co-operation is harder to acquire the less well you know the people being recorded so that your family or fellow students are likely to be the most co-operative. The more professional your approach is, the more helpful you will find people. If you are going to record strangers, you would be well advised to practise on your friends or your family first so that your technique means that the quality of what you record is good enough at the first attempt. It is embarrassing to go back to strangers to record their language a second time because your technique was too amateurish the first time. It is also important to remember that it is not considered ethical to record people **without their knowledge**.

There are several advantages in recording members of your family or close friends. They are likely to represent different generations and different genders; they may also have different levels of educational attainment. They are likely to be co-operative and they should be available for recording at almost any time.

Furthermore, as they know you they are likely to be more relaxed in their language use than strangers would be. In any case, you may be able to leave the recorder going for several days so that your family become used to it and gradually revert to their normal language which they might initially make more formal as soon as the tape recorder is switched on. A tape recorder is a 'stranger' in the house and most speakers adopt a more formal register until they have got used to it and treat it as a member of the family.

Another advantage is that any project you undertake by recording the members of your family or friends is likely to be unique in that no one else will be able to use that material because they will not have access to it. You also need to remember that if you record friends or strangers they may move suddenly out of your area and so not be available for checking and confirmation of certain details.

Your project may be quite different: it may be a historical study in which you want to consider English from some time ago. Here naturally it is important not only to have the text available, but to have some idea of how the text has been **treated** if it is available only in a modern edition. Many editors of older texts modernise the punctuation and some modernise the spelling. If the available edition did that, you would be able to use such a text only for a study of the vocabulary or of the syntax. You can go to your local record office and see if they will make an original text available to you, though you would then have the problem of reading the text, because older handwriting can present real difficulties to modern readers.

The possible ways of taking stock about the availability of data are only quoted as examples. There are many types of possible data and it is hardly surprising that many projects are based on written material from the last thirty or so years. But remember that restricting your choice to the most obvious type of data does not necessarily make a project any easier to accomplish.

The researcher

Finally, to take stock means taking stock of **yourself**: what are your own interests and abilities?

• If you have a poor ear and find tape recorders frightening, you would be silly to embark on a project involving sounds. Equally, if you have not been taught the phonetic alphabet and been given some practice in transcribing sounds using this alphabet, you may be well advised not to tackle a project describing or differentiating people's pronunciation. If you find syntax tedious, then you might consider investigating some other aspect of language.

But don't underestimate your abilities and don't forget that one of the best ways of learning about some aspect of language is to do a project on it. Consider carefully what interests you, because your project will take up a considerable amount of your time, and any project is better if it is motivated by enthusiasm and interest. Remember that certain types of projects may involve statistics because of the nature of the data and if that should be the case think over your attitude to statistics. Have you had any previous training or experience in statistics? Do you want to find out something about statistics, and are help and advice readily available to you? The level of statistical knowledge you require may not be very high so do not run away from a project just because some statistics may be needed.

THE TOPIC: DATA AND PURPOSE

Once you have taken stock, you are then faced with the problem of **choosing the topic** you will research for your project.

There are two aspects to your choice to take into account: what data you are going to use and what you want to use the data **for**. As far as possible you should keep these two in mind at the same time, for if you do not you may find yourself in some difficulties. For example, if you think only in terms of what data you might collect, you may say to yourself 'I will examine a copy of the *Beano* from this year and one from ten years ago'. But when you have both copies of the *Beano*, you may then be at a loss to know what you are going to do with them because you have not thought out the purpose for which you chose two copies of this comic.

On the other hand, you may decide you want to compare the level of attainment reached by a two-year old with that of a three-year old and then discover that it is impossible to find two children of these ages with roughly the same social backgrounds which would make such a comparison meaningful.

These two examples illustrate the common mistake of thinking of only one aspect of the choice of topic and then of finding that it is difficult to undertake the project because the other aspect of the choice of topic makes it impossible to accomplish. Now we have made that point we need to look at each aspect in turn.

• In considering the data you are going to collect you need a topic which is **not too large** so that you do not become overwhelmed by data. If you want to give a fairly comprehensive account of some piece of language, you will need a fairly small passage to make that possible. If you have a small passage it cannot be comprehensive for many aspects of language will not be found in it. If you analyse the style of a single poem by Hardy, it will not necessarily be typical of all Hardy's poetry, but this does not matter as long as you do not claim it is. A small passage is like a snapshot of the language which can focus only on a particular piece of language at one time. If you want to analyse a particular aspect of language, such as the choice of vocabulary, you will need a longer stretch of language to make sure that you can extract sufficient data.

There is no hard and fast rule as to how much data to collect or how much material to examine to provide a sufficient sample. To some extent the amount you need is determined by the purpose to which you wish to put the data. It is accepted that the data you collect can never be comprehensive, but you should have some general principles to guide you in the collection.

• The purpose for which a project may be undertaken is likely to be either **descriptive** or **theoretical**.

A descriptive project is one for which the theoretical position is already well established and the project will simply confirm the existing picture by reporting new data. Thus the general lines of child acquisition of language are already well defined and if you choose to write an account of the development of a child's language it would probably illustrate the currently accepted position by providing new information. All projects at your level are likely to be of this type.

A theoretical project is one where you choose data which you think will revise current thinking about a particular linguistic problem. You may think current views of child acquisition of language are flawed and seek to provide data to change those views. Clearly to do so you would need a good knowledge of current theories and some understanding of the possible data you could collect to make this approach feasible. Even if you embark on a descriptive project, the data you collect may not fit current views very well, and so you may be forced to question existing theories.

• In thinking about the purpose of a language project you should assume that language study is based on **contrast**, and it is as well to be clear about this implicit bias from the start. When you describe a piece of discourse you will notice first those aspects of it where it differs from the language you are familiar with, whether that is the standard language or some variety of it.

If you were describing the style of a poem you would probably not pay much attention to those sentences which have the order subject – verb – object (**SVO**), but you would to those sentences which had the order **SOV**. In looking at a child's language development you would probably assume that the child's language was a stage towards the acquisition of Standard English and you would notice those examples which seemed to mark stages towards the acquisition of adult patterns of syntax. If you were looking at an example of non-standard English you would notice where the vocabulary, syntax and sounds differed from Standard English.

It is difficult to avoid thinking in contrastive terms and to use Standard English as an implicit standard against which to judge other varieties of language. For many projects it may not matter too much that this bias exists, but you should be aware of it and you may need to take steps to reduce its importance. In discussing the style of a poem it is as significant to note how much of the language is standard and how much is not, because the amount of 'standardness' is an important aspect of the impact it creates. You should also avoid the idea that it is only worth describing 'deviant' types of language as though speakers of non-standard varieties are inherently more interesting to study than speakers of Received Pronunciation.

• Having taken stock you should know something about your interests and the material and help available to you. Think first about what area of language you might be interested in: stylistics, historical change, sociolinguistics or whatever. Choose a broad area that interests you and then think within it what purpose you wish to follow up and what data might best achieve that purpose.

This will involve reading about that subject and perhaps doing some practice in collecting data. For example, you might decide you are interested in the general area of vocabulary and would like to study new words and new meanings coming into the language. You could then look at some books on semantics, the growth of the English vocabulary, word-formation and dictionaries to give yourself the background in this area.

You would then choose which data you would pick. This could be either spoken such as found on television programmes or among your friends or written such as newspapers or novels. If you choose newspapers, you might want to look at several newspapers in a trial run to decide whether you would choose several copies of a single newspaper or single copies of several newspapers. You would need to practise picking up new words and meanings, which is not as easy as you might suppose, for trying to define what is meant by 'new' could be a problem.

The purpose of your project might be mainly descriptive, to outline those new words and meanings in your source, and partly theoretical, to decide whether the types of word and meaning being introduced matched those that current views suggested were likely. You will need to think of the new words and meanings as falling into various categories, which could be grammatical or semantic. In grammar you may distinguish between word categories like noun and verb, and within each category different types such as verb or phrasal verb (i.e. a verb consisting of at least two elements such as 'sit in'). In semantics you may distinguish what field of reference the words belong to, technology, business or domestic, for example. Or you may distinguish the words by register, such as slang, informal or formal English. The implicit contrast referred above is present in the distinction between new and old; it may also be present in the sense of what is now accepted compared with what was not accepted previously, since some words may only now have been seen in print.

COLLECTING THE DATA

The purpose for which you collect the data and the way in which you intend to **display it** should guide the way in which you collect and analyse it.

- You must be prepared for one or two false starts, and this is why a trial run is beneficial. If you collect new words from newspapers, you must first pick your newspapers. Then take a xerox as your working copy. Then decide what categories you will group your new words and meanings into and highlight in different colours each category you have chosen. Some words you may have to discard when you look into dictionaries and other records, because they are not new.

This same principle of choosing your material and then deciding which categories within it you will examine can be applied to most projects. If you study the differences in syntax between a non-standard text and a standard text, you would need to choose your texts and then decide what features to examine. Having chosen the features, you would then go through each text marking the different features in a way which allowed you to pick them out separately afterwards.

The arrangement of the data into categories is not as easy as you may assume. Language is never so straightforward as one might wish, and it is not always easy to decide to which category a word or a syntactic feature belongs. What is important is that the reasons and the methodology you have followed are clear not only to yourself but also to others. The various stages on the way to your final conclusions should be transparent.

• Once you have gone through your text and made a provisional choice of data and grouped it into various categories, you need to check each example to make sure that your provisional categorisation is justifiable so that you can discard or regroup those examples which do not fit your criteria. Some forms may fit more than one category and then you must decide which category to put a form in or whether it should go into both. Once you have gathered your data and arranged it into categories, you are in a position to analyse it and to think about writing up your project.

THE FINAL FORM OF A PROJECT

Most written reports of a project will include the following sections, though some sections may be amalgamated and others broken down into two or more parts.

Review of the research area and its background literature

In a project of this type it is not practical, or usually possible, to review all the literature in the research area you are working in.

What you should seek to do is to review the general position in the area of research you are working in by giving a resumé of one or two of the standard books about it. This will set the scene for your own project and allow the reader to see how you think what you are going to do fits into the **general view** of that area today.

You will choose those books whose focus is particularly directed towards the kind of topic you have chosen and provides a satisfactory background to it. If you are studying the vocabulary of Pepys's *Diary*, to review books on the history of English will not be very helpful. What you will need to do is to look at works which consider the English vocabulary in the seventeenth century and also those which deal with Pepys himself, since the vocabulary he used is bound to be affected by the sort of man he was and his interests.

Outline of the research topic

The review described in the previous paragraphs should lead naturally to what it is you are going to do. You need to give a clear statement of your **aims** and the **purpose** of your project.

Methodology

This section should state what method you have chosen to meet the aims of your project. Specify what **material** you have chosen and **why**; how you set about **extracting** the data from the material; how you divided the data into **categories** and what **problems** this may have caused; and finally how you intend to **analyse** and set out the data.

The data and its analysis

This will be the major section, particularly if your project is a descriptive one. On pp. 154–5 we advised about collecting the data, but what you are left with there may be described as 'raw data'. It will not usually be desirable to include the raw data in this analysis section; it will often be included as part of an **appendix** so that those who want to check your results against the raw data can do so.

In this analysis section you will include the data in a tabulated or grouped form. You will probably present each category in turn providing the overall figures, commenting on interesting or difficult cases, and concluding with a summative analysis. If you are studying new words and meanings in a newspaper, you could divide the data into two major categories: words and meanings. Each major category would then be sub-divided into such sub-categories as technical words, etc. according to the scheme you have adopted. Depending on the number of words you may be able to comment on each word in each sub-category, but a table giving the overall picture of new words and new meanings would also help to make your results more transparent. You could naturally also discuss the balance of categories of new words and meanings in your results.

General conclusions

This section pulls the whole project together so what you have done fits into what has already been done by others and what could be done in the future. Match your results against the background of the research area outlined in your opening review. How do your results compare with what one might have expected from your background reading? What points need special emphasis? To what extent do your results suggest additional topics that could be investigated?

Bibliography

The books and articles you have read and consulted should be listed here. It is simplest to list them in alphabetical order of the author's surname. The minimum information required is author's name, date of book, title of book, place of publication and publisher, as in the following example:

Blake, N.F. (1988) *Traditional English Grammar and Beyond*, London: Macmillan.

There are several ways in which this bibliographical information can be set out, but the advantage of doing it as suggested above is that if you have footnotes, you can refer to the books in a shorthand way by noting author's surname and date (e.g. Blake, 1988) because the reader will know the full reference is in the bibliography.

CONCLUSION

It is not possible to give an outline of all possible language research topics, and even less to suggest what topics could be tackled. We have spent much of our space on taking stock because a successful topic is one which matches your own interests, your own abilities and the resources and equipment you have available. What we have written here should enable you to approach your chosen topic with confidence. Good luck.

Glossary of Linguistic Terms

accent	Often used to refer to distinctive pronunciations which differ from that of Received Pronunciation
	It differs from dialect which includes syntax and vocabulary as well
acronym	A word formed from the initial letters of the words which make up a name, e.g. NATO (from North Atlantic Treaty Organisation)
active	A clause in which the subject is the actor of the verb; in a **passive** clause the actor is not the grammatical subject; see p. 14
addressee	The person being addressed or spoken to in any form of discourse
adjective	In traditional grammar a word which describes a noun, as *happy* in 'the *happy* man'; an adjective phrase is a group of one or more words fulfilling the function of an adjective; see p. 11
adverb	In traditional grammar a word which describes a verb; in 'he ran slowly', *slowly* describes how he ran
	An adverb phrase is a group of one or more words fulfilling the function of an adverb; see p. 11
affix	A morpheme which is attached to another word as an inflection or for derivation
	Affixes include prefixes at the beginning of a word and suffixes at the end of a word, e.g. *un-god-ly* with prefix *un-* and suffix *-ly*
	A derivational affix is used to form a new word, e.g. the suffix *-less* with *hope* gives the new word *hopeless*; an inflectional affix marks grammatical relations, in *comes*, the *-s* marks third person singular present indicative

159

alliteration   The repetition of the same sound at the beginning of two or more words in close proximity, e.g. 'time and tide'

alveolar   In phonetics the sounds formed by the tongue closing the air passage at the alveolar ridge (immediately behind the front top teeth)

    Such sounds in English include /t/, /d/, and /n/

analogy   The tendency to make all examples of a particular feature follow a regular pattern; thus since most nouns in English form their plural by adding -s, the tendency is for nouns which do not form their plural in this way to change by analogy to this plural, e.g. *formulas* compared with older *formulae*

article   In traditional grammar the name given to *a* or *an* (indefinite article) and to *the* (definite article)

assimilation   The process whereby two adjacent sounds become more alike in pronunciation because one of them discards those sound elements which are different from the elements found in the other; see pp. 33–4

auxiliary   A verb which is part of the verb phrase, but is not the head of the verb phrase except through elision; examples include *do, can, may, must, shall*; see p. 8

bilabial   In phonetics the sounds, such as /p/ and /b/, caused by closing both lips and then opening them quickly

bilingual   Proficiency in two languages, usually as a native speaker

clause   A clause normally consists of a subject and a verb, though it may have other elements as well

    Clauses can be linked together through co-ordination, i.e. when they are of the same status, or subordination, i.e. when one is of higher rank than the other; see pp. 15–17

code switching   The change from one language or variety of language to another within a conversation

A speaker in Belgium might change from French to Flemish and back again depending on the subject matter and the other participants in the conversation

collocation   The habitual co-occurrence of two words

command   A type of sentence which is an order, e.g. 'Go away'; also known as an imperative

Such sentences normally have no subject; see p. 19

complement   An adjective, noun phrase or a clause acting as a noun phrase which is dependent on a stative verb

In 'He is happy', the adjective *happy* is the complement

complex sentence   A sentence consisting of at least one subordinate clause in addition to the main clause, i.e. the clause which can stand on its own; see p. 18

compound   A word consisting of at least two free morphemes, i.e. two elements which are themselves words as in *freewheel*, where *free* and *wheel* are both words

compound sentence   A sentence of at least two main clauses joined together through co-ordination, as 'He sat down and the seat collapsed'. see pp. 17–18

conjunction   A conjunction can be either co-ordinate or subordinate

A co-ordinate conjunction joins together elements of equal rank, as the two adjectives in 'a rare and auspicious event' are joined by *and*

A subordinate conjunction usually joins a subordinate clause to a main clause, e.g. *if, when, although*; see p. 10 and pp. 17–19

connotation   The associations attached to a word in addition to its dictionary definition; e.g. in addition to its colour meaning, *white* has the connotation of purity

co-ordination	The joining together of two linguistic elements of equal weight; see **conjunction**
correlative	Two clauses linked together by two conjunctions or adverbs which function as a pair to reinforce the logical relationship between them, as in '*Though* she is beautiful, *nevertheless* she is not proud'
creole	A pidgin which has been adopted as the mother tongue of some people
determiner	A word that occurs before the head, or premonifiers if any, in a noun phrase, such as *the* or *my*; only one determiner can appear before a premodifier or head; see pp. 9–10
dialect	A variety of language associated with a particular speech community, either geographically to give a regional dialect or socially to give a class dialect
diphthong	A vowel sound in which there is a change of quality during its articulation and is represented graphically by the first and last point of articulation to suggest that it contains two vowel sounds, e.g. /aɪ/.
diglossia	A situation in which two significantly different states of a single language are both used by a speech community
discourse	The organisation of language beyond the sentence
dynamic	A verb which expresses an action rather than a state and can take forms in *-ing* as part of the progressive, e.g. *come, is coming*
ellipsis	The omission of some part of the sentence which can be understood from the context

In the answer 'Yes, he is' to the question 'Is he coming?', the present participle *is coming* is reduced through ellipsis to *is* |
| **euphemism** | A term regarded as more acceptable socially which has replaced another term which has become tainted by the unfavourable associations of the concept it refers to

Hence to *spend a penny* is a euphemism |

exclamation   A sentence which expresses surprise, amaze-ment, etc. and is usually followed by an exclamation mark, as in 'What a wonderful day!' see p. 19

finite   A term used to describe those parts of the verb which are marked for tense, person and number; see p. 13

fricative   In phonetics a term used of consonants which are produced through constricting some part of the air passage, e.g. /f/ and /s/.

grammaticalisation   The process whereby what had been an optional feature in a language becomes a regular feature of its grammar

In English questions it used to be possible to say either *Came he?* or *Did he come?* (i.e. with or without a part of the verb *to do*), but today the *do* form has been grammaticalised and questions now include the *do* auxiliary reg-ularly

head   The obligatory element of a phrase on which all the other elements depend. In the noun phrase 'the happy man', *man* is the head and both *the* and *happy* are dependent on it

homonym   Two words which are identical in speech and writing

infinitive   Equivalent to the base form of a verb which is entered in dictionaries as the headword; it can also be used with *to*: *(to) come; (to) enter*

inflection   The marking of grammatical categories like case or tense through the use of an affix or some other linguistic mechanism

interjection   A word in traditional grammar which stands outside the normal grammar of a sentence, e.g. 'Damn! she's not coming', see p. 11

inversion   Reversing the order of two elements, as for example the order of the subject and verb is reversed to form a question so that *He did come* becomes *Did he come?*

language contact   The situation in which two or more languages come into contact with one another on a regular basis and force their speakers to adopt some strategy such as the development of a pidgin to enable communication to take place

lexis   The term used to describe the vocabulary of a language

liquid   In phonetics referring to /r/ and /l/, but often taken to include /w/ and /j/ sounds as well

modal   A closed class of verbs which are part of the auxiliary verbs and express such features as obligation and necessity; they include *can*, *may* and *shall* and are used with a lexical verb; see p. 8

morpheme   The smallest distinctive unit of meaning in grammar

A free morpheme can stand by itself as a word, e.g. *boy*, but a bound morpheme must be attached to another morpheme, e.g. the *-s* in *boys*; see **affix**, and pp. 3–5

morphology   The study of morphemes

nasal   In phonetics the term used of sounds which are produced by air coming both through the mouth and the nasal passage, e.g. /n/.

non-finite   Those parts of the verb which are not marked for tense, person or number such as the infinitive and participle

A non-finite verb cannot act by itself as a predicator; see p. 13

noun   In traditional grammar the name given to a person, place or thing; see pp. 5–6

noun phrase   A phrase that acts like a noun and can fulfil the role of subject or object

object   A noun phrase which suffers the action of a transitive verb and usually follows the verb in order

onomatopoeia   The term used to refer to those words which are said to replicate natural sounds, e.g. *woof-woof* as the noise made by a dog

palatal   In phonetics the sounds made when the central part of the tongue is raised to touch the hard palate, e.g. /j/.

participle   A non-finite part of the verb used as an adjective or in the verb phrase after auxiliaries

Present participles end in *-ing*, e.g. *coming*, and past participles end in *-en* or *-(e)d/t*, e.g. *given, learned/learnt*

passive   see **active**

phoneme   The minimal unit in the sound system of a language which can be tested through substitution: if the sound changes the meaning of a word when it replaces another sound, then both are phonemes. Thus /**f**/ and /**c**/ are phonemes because *fat* and *cat* have different meanings

phonetic alphabet   As the Roman alphabet does not contain enough letters, a special alphabet has been developed to represent the sounds of any language

The standard form of this alphabet is known as the International Phonetic Alphabet. The characters used to represent English sounds are listed on pp. 20–1

phonetics   The study of the sounds which can be made by humans

phonology   The study of the sounds of a single language

phrase   A group of one or more words, usually without a finite verb; see pp. 11–14

pidgin   A means of communication developed through language contact which is usually a simplified linguistic system of a single language with inputs from one or more other languages

It is no one's mother tongue

plosive   In phonetics the sounds made when the air passage is completely blocked for a moment (usually by the lips); when unblocked the air escapes as though with an 'explosive' sound; examples are /**p**/ and /**b**/.

postmodifier   Those parts of the noun phrase which come after the head; in English most usually a relative clause or prepositional phrase: in 'the boy with the big head', *with the big head* is the postmodifier which comes after *boy* (head); see pp. 11–12

predicator The verb phrase which is an obligatory constituent of a clause; see p. 12

prefix see **affix**

premodifier Those parts of the noun phrase which come after the determiner and before the head; in 'the beautiful red house', *beautiful red* comes after *the* (determiner) and before *house* (head); see p. 11

preposition A word such as *in*, *on* or *by* which comes before a noun phrase to express the relationship of that phrase to the rest of the clause; in the prepositional phrase 'on the table', *on* is the preposition and *the table* is the noun phrase; see p. 10

progressive A form of the verb formed by a part of the auxiliary *to be* and the present participle of a lexical verb to express an action which is continuing as in 'he is coming'; see pp. 13–14

pronoun In traditional grammar a term used of a closed class of words that can stand in place of a noun; see pp. 6–7

psycholinguistics The study of the relation between linguistic behaviour and the psychological processes such as mind or memory which are assumed to determine it

question A type of sentence which asks a question and is sometimes referred to as an interrogative; in English questions normally have inversion of subject and (auxiliary) verb; e.g. 'Is he coming?' see pp. 18–19

rankshift A term describing the process whereby a linguistic unit is used lower down the grammatical hierarchy. Hence a word like *free* can be used as a morpheme in *freewheel*, and a clause like *he is coming* can be used as a phrase in *I think he is coming*

Received Pronunciation The prestige variety of speech associated with education and high social status

register	A variety of language which is employed in relation to the social environment in which it is used, e.g. formal or informal
rhetoric	The way of organising an utterance or speech to achieve the effect on the listener one intends which was promoted and codified in the past; nowadays it is particularly associated with figures of speech such as metaphor and simile
sentence	In traditional grammar a unit of language consisting of one or more clauses and in writing marked off by a capital letter at the beginning and a fullstop at the end; see pp. 17–19
slang	Colourful colloquial usage often associated with particular groups of people, though the slang of one age may become accepted as standard in the next
sociolinguistics	The study of the relation between linguistic usage and social situations and structures
standard language	That variety of language which cuts across regional differences and has become institutionalised as the status variety to be used in writing, education, government, etc.; see p. xi
statement	A type of sentence which makes a statement and is also referred to as declarative
	It is often regarded as the normative sentence in a language and in English has the order subject-verb-object/complement; see p. 18
stative	A verb which expresses a state rather than an action, e.g. 'I *am* happy'.
subject	A noun phrase which is normally the actor of the verb and precedes the verb in statements; see p. 15
subjunctive	No longer an important mood in English, but traditionally it represented something hypothetical such as a wish
	In the present tense it is recognised by the absence of final -*s* in the third person singular, e.g. 'Long *live* the Queen'; it is today more

usually expressed through modal auxiliaries, e.g. 'I wish he *would come*'.

subordinate clause   A clause which cannot stand alone as it is dependent on another clause and is usually introduced by a subordinate conjunction

In the sentence 'When he comes I will tell him', *When he comes* cannot make a complete sentence; see p. 18

suffix   see **affix**

syntax   The study of the grammatical relations of a language, which in English are principally expressed through word order

token   In vocabulary this refers to the number of times a lexical item or type occurs

transitive   A verb which requires an object; its opposite is intransitive

type   In vocabulary this refers to the different lexical items which may be counted

We refer to 'lexical items' rather than 'words', because *sing* and *sings*, although different words, are the same lexical item

velar   In phonetics the sounds produced when the back of the tongue is in contact with the soft palate or velum

verb   A lexical verb differs from an auxiliary in having meaning in itself

A verb like *sing* is a lexical verb because it means something by itself, whereas an auxiliary like *shall* is used in conjunction with a lexical verb

voice   A sound is said to be voiced if the vocal cords vibrate as it is pronounced; it is otherwise unvoiced

If you place a finger on your Adam's apple you will feel the vibration for /z/ (voiced), but not for /s/ (unvoiced).

word

Words can be divided into two types *lexical* and *grammatical*

Lexical words are usually nouns, adjectives, adverbs and verbs and contain significant meaning in themselves, whereas grammatical words such as prepositions and articles are important in the organisation and structure of a sentence

Suggestions for Further Reading

For further information about **grammar** the following books are useful: N.F. Blake, *Traditional English Grammar and Beyond* (London: Macmillan, 1988); Geoffrey Leech, Margaret Deuchar and Robert Hoogenraad, *English Grammar for Today: A New Introduction* (London: Macmillan, 1982) and Dennis Freeborn, *A Course Book in English Grammar* (London: Macmillan, 1987). A book which includes phonology is Barbara Strang, *Modern English Structure*, 2nd edn (London: Arnold, 1968). A book on phonology is Charles W. Kreidler, *The Pronunciation of English: A Course Book in Phonology* (Oxford: Blackwell, 1989).

An entertaining introduction to **child language** is David Crystal, *Listen to your Child: A Parent's Guide to Children's Language* (London: Penguin, 1986). See also Jerome Bruner, *Child's Talk, Learning to Use Language* (London: Oxford University Press, 1983), Jill and Peter de Villiers, *Language Acquisition* (Cambridge MA: Havard University Press, 1978) and Gordon Wells, *The Meaning Makers* (London: Hodder & Stoughton, 1987).

On **language change** see Jean Aitchison, *Language Change: Progress or Decay?* (London: Fontana, 1981). For histories of English see A.C. Baugh and T. Cable, *A History of the English Language*, 3rd edn (London: Routledge & Kegan Paul, 1978), Dick Leith, *A Social History of English* (London: Routledge & Kegan Paul, 1983), and David Burnley, *The History of the English Language: A Source Book* (London: Longman, 1992).

The number of books on **language variety and the social context** is enormous, and the recommendations here are very selective. On standard language see J. and L. Milroy, *Authority in Language: Investigating Language Prescription and Standardisation*, 2nd edn (London: Routledge & Kegan Paul, 1989) and Sidney Greenbaum, *Good English and the Grammarian* (London: Longman, 1988). General books include Dennis Freeborn with David Langford and Peter French, *Varieties of English: An Introduction to the Study of Language* (London: Macmillan, 1986), W.R. O'Donnell and Loreto Todd, *Variety in Contemporary English*, 2nd edn (London: Allen & Unwin, 1989), and Randolph Quirk and Gabriele Stein, *English in Use* (London: Longman, 1990). See also E. Ryan and H. Giles, *Attitudes* *towards Language Variation* (London: Arnold 1982), P. Trudgill, *Sociolinguistics: An Introduction,* (Harmondsworth: Penguin, 1974), and Lesley Milroy, *Language and Social Networks* 2nd edn (Oxford: Blackwell, 1987).

A book which explores some of the attitudes linked with **accent** is John Honey, *Does Accent Matter?* (London: Faber, 1989).

On **language and styles** see D. Crystal and D. Davy, *Investigating English Style* (London: Longman, 1969), M. Stubbs, *Discourse Analysis* (Oxford: Blackwell, 1983), N.F. Blake, *An Introduction to the Language of Literature* (London: Macmillan, 1990) and Ronald Carter and Walter Nash, *Seeing through Language: A Guide to Styles of English Writing* (Oxford: Blackwell, 1990).

For help with your **project** you can consult Christine McDonald, *English Language Project Work* (London: Macmillan, 1992).

For a **general book on language** see David Crystal, *The Cambridge Encyclopedia of Language* (Cambridge: Cambridge University Press, 1987).

The recently published *The Oxford Companion to the English Language,* edited by Tom McArthur (Oxford: Oxford University Press, 1992) contains a wealth of information and ideas, some of which could be followed up as projects.

Dwight Bolinger, *Language, the Loaded Weapon: the Use and Abuse of Language Today* (London: Longman, 1980) discusses the influence of language on thinking and behaviour.

Index

abbreviations 60, 65, 72, 103, 107–8, 130
Academie Française 84
accent 90, 92, 105, 159
acronym 103, 159
action 8–9, 12–14, 122
active 14, 27, 118, 159
Adelmann, Mr 127
addressee 159
adjectival phrase 11, 122
adjective 4–5, 8–9, 11, 17, 38, 41–2, 47, 50, 62, 68, 70, 73, 80, 96, 101, 118, 137, 159, 161, 165; comparative 9, 42; superlative 9
adverb(ial) 5, 9, 11–12, 15–18, 27, 43–4, 50, 67–8, 73–4, 100, 107 110, 116–18, 122, 138, 159, 162; of manner 9; of place 9, 15, 43, 68; of time 9, 116, 138
adverbial phrase 11, 68, 159
advertisement 113–15
advertising 19
affix 159, 163–4, 166
affricate 22–4
Age of Reason 57
agent 45, 47, 51
alliteration 115, 118, 138, 160
alveolar 22, 32, 160
Alzheimer's 128, 130–1
America(n) 35, 39, 59, 83, 90, 92, 95
ampersand 65, 72
analogy 42, 54, 160
Anglo-Saxons 82
antonym 116
apostrophe 6
archaism 63, 66, 70
article 9, 67, 160
articulation 22–4, 33
aspect 12–14
assimilation 33–4, 160
audience xii, 107–8, 110, 119, 123, 126–9, 131–2
Austin, Frances 71

Austin Allegro Owners Workshop Manual 110
Australian 90–1
auxiliary 8, 12–14, 18–19, 26, 44–5, 47–8, 50, 69, 74, 96, 160, 165–6, 168; modal 8, 12–13, 26, 61, 109–10, 125, 127, 138, 164, 168; primary 8, 12–13, 15, 26

Bangladeshi 91
Beano 151
Belgium 161
Bernstein, Basil 95
bilabial 22, 31, 34, 160
bilingualism 93–4, 160
Birmingham 87
Black English Vernacular (BEV) 95–7
Blake, N.F. 157
Bodmin (Cornwall) 71
Bolinger, Dwight 103
borrowing 6, 57, 63, 70
brackets 60
Britain 116, 128
British Empire 58, 79

Canterbury Tales, The 64, 82
capital letter 5, 17, 19, 60, 65, 67, 118
Caxton, W. 64–71, 73, 75
Chalmers-Hunt, B. L. 110
Chaucer, Geoffrey 64–71, 82
China 93
Christ 70
Clare, Professor Anthony 128–32
clause 2–3, 11, 15–18, 26, 42, 45, 50, 60–1, 66–9, 80, 107–8, 110, 121–2, 160–2, 166–8; main 10, 74, 161; relative 7, 28, 117, 165; subordinate 18, 75, 161, 168; superordinate 126, 138
Clift, Elizabeth 71–3; Robert 71; William 71–6